P.O.W.E.R. UP!

5 Habits to Improve Your Writing

BRADLEY C. THOMPSON, EdD, PhD

innovo
PUBLISHING
innovopublishing.com

Published by Innovo Publishing, LLC
www.innovopublishing.com
1-888-546-2111

innovo
PUBLISHING
Innovopublishing.com

Innovo Publishing LLC is a Christ-centered publisher located near Memphis, TN. Since 2008, Innovo has published quality books, eBooks, audiobooks, music, screenplays, and online and physical curricula that support the Great Commission, equip believers, and help create a positive Christian worldview. Innovo's capabilities and global reach provide Christian authors, artists, and ministries access to the world for Christ. To learn more about Innovo Publishing, visit our website at innovopublishing.com. To connect with other Christian creatives and to learn best practices for creating, publishing, marketing, and selling Christian titles, visit the Christian Publishing Portal at cpportal.com.

P.O.W.E.R. Up!
5 Habits to Improve Your Writing

Unless otherwise noted, all Scripture was taken from the New American Standard Bible®, Copyright © 1960, 1971, 1977, 1995, 2020 by The Lockman Foundation. All rights reserved.

ISBN: 979-8-88928-135-1

Cover Design & Interior Layout: Innovo Publishing, LLC

Printed in the United States of America
U.S. Printing History
First Edition: 2025

CONTENTS

INTRODUCTION & OBJECTIVES

Welcome to *P.O.W.E.R. Up! 5 Habits to Improve Your Writing*. Whether you're an experienced writer looking to refine your skills or someone who struggles to get words onto the page, this booklet is designed to help you navigate the writing process with confidence and clarity.

Developed from the *P.O.W.E.R. Up!* course taught by Dr. Bradley Thompson, this guide breaks down the five fundamental skills necessary for effective writing: *planning, organizing, writing, editing, and revising—P-O-W-E-R!* These essential steps, often overlooked or rushed through, are the building blocks of successful academic and professional writing. By strengthening each of these areas, you'll not only produce stronger papers but also develop habits that will improve your overall communication.

This booklet serves as both a roadmap and a practical toolkit. It provides structured guidance, practical exercises, and key strategies to help you craft a well-researched, clearly written, and polished paper. Whether you're writing a term paper, a research article, or any formal written work, *P.O.W.E.R. Up!* will walk you through each stage of the writing process, ensuring that your final product meets high academic and professional standards.

By the time you complete this guide, you'll have a deeper understanding of how to approach writing as a *process*—one that involves careful planning, thoughtful structuring, and meticulous revision. Most importantly, you'll have the tools to create clear, concise, and compelling written work.

Effective writing is more than just putting words on a page—it requires careful thought, structured organization, and well-supported arguments. *P.O.W.E.R. Up!* is designed to provide you with the essential tools for successful written communication, ensuring that you can approach any writing task with confidence and skill.

This booklet focuses on three key objectives that form the foundation of effective writing:

1. *Understanding writing principles:* A strong writer must first understand the core principles that shape academic and professional writing. This includes mastering research methodologies, recognizing different writing styles, and developing a structured approach to composing clear and coherent papers. By strengthening these foundational skills, you will be better prepared to craft compelling and well-organized written work.

2. *Identifying key elements of paper production:* Every well-written paper is built upon essential components that guide the reader through a logical and persuasive argument. You will learn to,

    »   develop a clear and focused thesis statement,
    »   structure your arguments in a way that enhances readability and impact, and
    »   integrate credible sources effectively to support your claims.

    By recognizing these crucial elements, you will be able to write with greater clarity and purpose, producing papers that are both engaging and academically sound.

3. *Applying research strategies:* Quality writing relies on thorough research and the ability to integrate scholarly sources effectively. You will explore research techniques that help you find, evaluate, and apply credible information to strengthen your arguments. Emphasis will be placed on proper citation methods, source evaluation, and ethical research practices to ensure that every paper meets academic integrity standards.

The *P.O.W.E.R. Up!* approach goes beyond theory by encouraging active participation and hands-on learning. You will engage in exercises that put these principles into practice, guiding you through the process of researching, drafting, editing, and revising your work. By applying the strategies outlined in this book, you will gain the confidence and skills needed to tackle any academic writing assignment successfully. You will not only understand what makes good writing but will also have the tools to produce well-researched, clearly written, and effectively structured papers.

Let's get started and build the skills that will *P.O.W.E.R. Up!* your writing!

Chapter One

PLAN YOUR PAPER

B y the end of this chapter, you will learn how to,

- Understand the importance of planning before writing.
- Choose a focused and manageable topic.
- Organize your initial thoughts using visual tools like clustering diagrams.

Begin with a Plan

Before you begin the process of writing a research paper, it is essential to start with a solid plan. Planning lays the foundation for an effective and well-structured paper, providing clear direction and ensuring that your work remains focused and organized. Without proper planning, writers often struggle with vague arguments, lack of coherence, and difficulty in completing the assignment on time. Taking the time to plan your paper will not only improve the quality of your writing but will also make the research and drafting process significantly easier.

In this chapter, we will explore the fundamental steps of planning a research paper, which include understanding the assignment requirements, choosing an appropriate topic, narrowing the focus, and using a cluster diagram to brainstorm ideas. By following these steps, you can alleviate much of the stress associated with writing and set yourself up for academic success.

Choose and Narrow a Topic

Selecting the right topic for your paper is a critical first step in the writing process. A well-chosen topic sets the foundation for effective research, clear argumentation, and an engaging discussion. If a topic is too broad, it can become overwhelming to cover effectively within the required length of the paper. On the other hand, if it is too narrow, you may struggle to find enough credible sources to support your analysis. Striking the right balance is essential for crafting a well-structured and compelling research paper.

Once you have chosen a general area, the next step is to refine your topic into a more focused subject. A broad topic, such as "The Reformation," covers a vast historical period with multiple theological, social, and political implications. Attempting to address all aspects of this topic in a single research paper would result in an unfocused and overly general discussion. Instead, consider narrowing your focus to a specific aspect of the Reformation, such as Martin Luther's 95 Theses and its impact on European religious structures. This more precise topic allows for deeper analysis, ensuring that your research remains well-organized and provides meaningful insights.

To effectively narrow your topic, ask yourself key questions: *What specific aspect of this topic interests me the most? Are there significant debates or controversies surrounding this subject? What key questions can I explore in my research? Is there sufficient scholarly material available to support my paper?* Answering these questions will help you refine your focus and develop a topic that is both manageable and researchable. By carefully selecting and narrowing your topic, you set yourself up for a more productive research and writing process, leading to a stronger and more impactful paper.

Use a Cluster Diagram to Generate Ideas

When starting a research paper, one of the biggest challenges can be organizing your thoughts and developing a clear focus.

A cluster diagram is an effective brainstorming tool that helps visually map out ideas, making it easier to see connections between different aspects of your topic. By using a cluster diagram, you can break down broad ideas into smaller, more manageable subtopics, ensuring that your research remains structured and well-organized.

To create a cluster diagram, begin by writing your main topic in the center of a blank page. This central topic represents the overall theme of your paper. From there, draw branches outward for major themes or secondary ideas related to the topic. These secondary ideas represent key aspects of the subject that will form the foundation of your research. Next, expand each secondary idea with tertiary ideas, which are specific details or supporting points that provide further depth to your topic.

For example, if your main topic is the Reformation, you can branch out as follows:

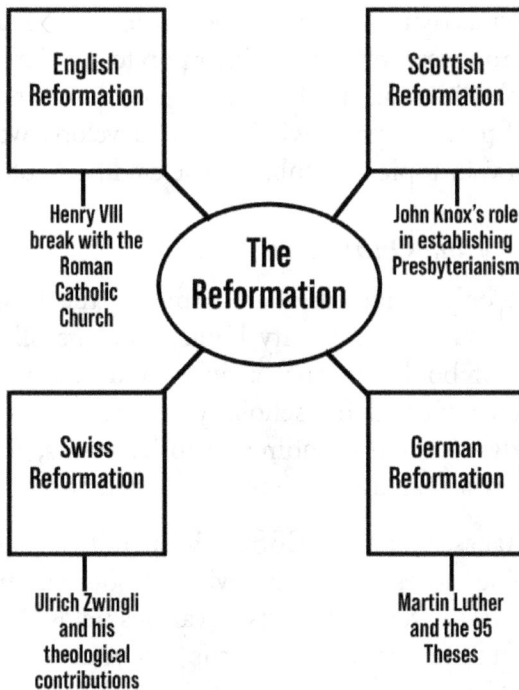

By structuring your ideas in this way, you create a clear roadmap for your research, making it easier to develop focused arguments and maintain coherence in your paper.

Using a cluster diagram allows you to visualize relationships between ideas, which can help refine your focus and highlight key themes to explore further. It also serves as a valuable organizational tool when gathering sources, as you can see which aspects require more research and which are well-supported. By investing time in this brainstorming process, you can ensure that your research is comprehensive and your writing remains structured and logical from the beginning to the final draft.

Research Your Topic

Once you have clearly defined your topic, the next step is to gather credible sources that will provide the foundation for your research paper. Effective research is essential for developing strong arguments, supporting claims with evidence, and ensuring the accuracy of your writing. Your research should incorporate a variety of sources, including books, journal articles, and reputable online resources. Using a mix of these materials will help you develop a well-rounded perspective on your topic and enhance the credibility of your paper.

Use the Library and Online Resources

Libraries and online databases are some of the best places to find academic sources. University library catalogs offer access to a wide range of books, journal articles, and research materials that have been reviewed for scholarly accuracy. These resources are particularly useful for finding historical texts, foundational theories, and critical analyses related to your subject.

Academic databases such as EBSCOhost, JSTOR, and Google Scholar provide access to peer-reviewed journal articles and academic papers written by experts in various fields. These sources offer high-quality research that can support your arguments with verified data and in-depth analysis. Additionally, Google Scholar and other academic search engines can help locate articles from trusted institutions, research organizations, and university publishers. When using online sources, always evaluate the credibility of the website and ensure that the information is from a reputable source rather than personal blogs or non-scholarly websites.

Conduct an Effective Online Search

To find the most relevant sources, you need to use effective online search strategies. Start by using specific keywords related to your topic. For example, instead of searching for "Reformation," which is too broad, try "German Reformation" or "Martin Luther's 95 Theses" to narrow your results. Using quotation marks around phrases such as "Martin Luther's 95 Theses" ensures that search engines return results containing the exact phrase rather than unrelated materials.

Another useful strategy is to filter results by date to find the most up-to-date research. Many academic databases allow you to adjust search settings to retrieve sources from a specific time period, ensuring that you are using the most current and relevant information. Additionally, reviewing the bibliographies of scholarly articles can lead you to other valuable sources, helping you build a more comprehensive research base.

By utilizing library catalogs, academic databases, and effective search techniques, you can gather the necessary information to develop a well-supported and thoroughly researched paper. Taking the time to find credible sources will strengthen your arguments, improve the overall quality of your work, and demonstrate academic integrity.

Apply Your Learning: Select a Topic and Gather Sources

Now that you understand the importance of planning, narrowing your topic, and conducting thorough research, it is time to apply what you have learned. The process of selecting a well-defined topic and gathering credible sources is essential for building a strong foundation for your research paper. By completing the following tasks, you will not only refine your research focus but also develop valuable skills in organization, critical thinking, and academic writing.

Step 1: Select a Specific Research Topic

The first step is to choose a specific research topic. While broad topics provide general direction, narrowing them down ensures that your research remains focused and manageable. For instance, rather than writing a paper on the Reformation as a whole, you could explore a specific aspect such as Martin Luther's 95 Theses and its influence on European religious structures. Selecting a precise topic allows for a more in-depth discussion and a stronger thesis statement.

To help refine your topic, consider asking yourself the following questions:

- What specific aspect of this topic interests me?
- Are there any debates or controversies within this subject?
- Is there enough scholarly research available to support my paper?

A well-chosen topic will not only make research easier but will also keep you engaged in the writing process.

Step 2: Create a Cluster Diagram

After selecting your topic, the next step is to create a cluster diagram to visually organize your ideas. A cluster diagram helps break down your topic into secondary ideas (major themes) and tertiary ideas (supporting details). This method allows you to see the relationships between different concepts and develop a logical structure for your paper. For example, if your topic is Martin Luther's 95 Theses, your secondary ideas might include,

- The historical context of the Reformation
- The main theological arguments in the 95 Theses
- The reaction of the Catholic Church
- The long-term effects on European religious structures

Under each secondary idea, you can list tertiary ideas that serve as specific points of discussion. This visual brainstorming process will guide your research and ensure that your paper remains structured and well-organized.

Step 3: Find and Submit Credible Sources

With a clear topic and structured outline, the next step is to gather at least ten credible sources that provide research and evidence for your paper. These sources should include a mix of,

- books (for foundational knowledge and in-depth discussion),
- peer-reviewed journal articles (for scholarly analysis and recent research), and
- academic websites (such as Google Scholar, university publications, or research institutions).

Using academic databases such as EBSCOhost, JSTOR, and Google Scholar, conduct targeted searches using specific keywords related to your topic. Filter results by date, relevance, and credibility to ensure that your research is current and reliable. This step will help you gather strong supporting material for your arguments.

Step 4: Write and Submit Five Citations with Summaries

Once you have collected your sources, the final step is to write five citations, each accompanied by a well-structured paragraph summarizing a source. These summaries should concisely explain,

- the main argument or thesis of the source,
- key findings or evidence presented, and
- how this source will contribute to your research paper.

For example, if you are writing about Martin Luther's 95 Theses, a summary might look like this:

Citation:
Smith, John. *The Reformation and Its Impact on Europe.* Oxford University Press, 2018.

Summary:

In this book, John Smith provides an in-depth analysis of how Martin Luther's 95 Theses sparked religious reform across Europe. He examines the political and social factors that influenced the Reformation and discusses the long-term consequences of Luther's actions. The book also highlights the role of printing technology in spreading Reformation ideas. This source will be valuable for my research because it provides historical context and supports my argument on the widespread influence of Luther's writings.

Final Thoughts

Completing these steps will ensure that you have a strong research foundation before moving into the writing phase. By carefully selecting a focused topic, organizing your ideas through a cluster diagram, gathering reliable sources, and summarizing key research materials, you will be well-prepared to develop a structured and compelling research paper.

Happy researching!

Chapter Two

CHOOSE AND NARROW A TOPIC

B y the end of this chapter, you will learn how to,

- Brainstorm and evaluate potential writing topics.
- Narrow broad ideas into specific, researchable questions.
- Select a topic that aligns with assignment goals and audience expectations.

Review

Before progressing further in the writing process, it is important to reflect on the foundational steps completed in the previous chapter. Reviewing past assignments allows you to assess your progress, identify any gaps in your research, and ensure that you are building a strong foundation for your paper. A well-planned and well-researched paper begins with carefully executed preparatory work.

By now, you should have chosen a research topic. Selecting a topic was a critical step, as it set the direction for your research and ensured that your paper remains focused and manageable. If your topic still feels too broad or lacks specificity, this is the perfect time to refine it further by narrowing your focus to a specific question or argument.

Additionally, you should have collected at least ten sources from a variety of credible materials, including books, journal articles, and reputable online sources. These sources will serve as the foundation of your research, providing the evidence and perspectives needed to support your claims. As you review your sources, consider whether they offer diverse viewpoints and whether they sufficiently address your research topic. If some sources seem less relevant, now is the time to seek additional materials that better align with your focus.

Finally, you should have created a cluster diagram to organize your ideas and visually map out the structure of your paper. This brainstorming tool helped you break down your topic into secondary and tertiary ideas, clarifying how different aspects of your research connect. Reviewing your cluster diagram will help you determine whether your paper has a logical structure and whether additional refinement is needed before moving forward.

Taking a moment to review these assignments ensures that you are fully prepared for the next phase of the writing process. If any of these foundational steps are incomplete or require adjustment, now is the ideal time to make necessary revisions before advancing to forming a research question and integrating citations effectively.

Introduction: Choose and Narrow a Topic

It's time to refine your research by focusing on two essential components: forming a research question and understanding citation. These elements are fundamental to developing a well-structured, academically rigorous paper. Equally important is the proper *use* of citations, which ensures academic integrity and prevents plagiarism. By the end of this chapter, you will gain a deeper understanding of how to craft an effective research question that serves as the foundation of your paper. You will also learn how to incorporate sources correctly through quotations, paraphrasing, and summarizing, ensuring that your research is both credible and ethically sound.

Form a Research Question and Understand Citation

Now that you have selected a research topic, organized your ideas, and gathered relevant sources, it is time to refine your research by focusing on two crucial aspects: forming a research question and understanding citations. These elements are fundamental to producing a well-structured, academically sound paper.

A well-crafted research question serves as the backbone of your paper. It provides clear direction, helping you avoid vague or unfocused writing. A strong research question guides your argument, informs your thesis statement, and ensures that your research remains relevant and purposeful. Without a clearly defined question, your paper may lack coherence, making it difficult to present a compelling argument or reach a meaningful conclusion.

Equally important is understanding citation and avoiding plagiarism. Academic integrity is a critical part of scholarly writing, and properly citing your sources ensures that you give credit to the original authors while supporting your arguments with credible research. Failure to cite sources correctly can lead to plagiarism, whether intentional or accidental, which can have serious academic consequences. Learning how to use citation styles such as MLA, APA, or Turabian will help you seamlessly integrate research into your writing while maintaining ethical writing practices.

By the end of this chapter, you will have a deeper understanding of how to formulate a strong research question that will shape your paper and how to incorporate sources correctly to enhance the credibility of your work. These skills will help you conduct structured research and develop a well-supported academic paper. Let's begin by exploring how to craft an effective research question.

Form a Research Question

A strong research question is the foundation of a well-structured and focused academic paper. It serves as a guiding framework that directs your research, shapes your thesis statement, and ensures that your writing remains purposeful and analytical. Without a clear research question, a paper can become disorganized, lacking depth and coherence. A well-crafted question not only clarifies what you are investigating but also determines the scope of your research and the direction of your argument.

When developing a research question, consider the following key characteristics:

- *Clarity and specificity:* Your question should be clearly stated and focused on a specific issue rather than vague or overly general.

- Researchability: Your question should be answerable using credible academic sources, including books, journal articles, and reputable online materials.

- Balanced scope: Your question should not be too broad, making it difficult to cover thoroughly within the given paper length, nor too narrow, limiting the availability of sources and depth of discussion.

- Invitation for analysis: A strong question should allow for critical thinking, discussion, and argumentation rather than simply prompting a yes-or-no answer or a basic factual summary.

Examples of Effective Research Questions

The following research questions are specific and researchable, and they encourage analytical discussion:

Theology paper:
How did the Council of Nicaea shape early Christian doctrine?

History paper:
What were the primary causes of the English Reformation?

Education paper:
How do teaching strategies differ between adult learners and children?

These questions guide the research process by defining the main topic while allowing for in-depth exploration and argumentation.

Once you have formulated your research question, begin organizing your research materials around answering that question. Group your sources according to how they contribute to different aspects of your argument. Identify key themes and patterns in the existing literature, and start developing a logical structure for presenting your findings. A strong research question not only provides direction but also enhances the overall clarity and persuasiveness of your writing, ensuring that your paper remains focused and impactful.

Understand Citation and Avoid Plagiarism

Academic writing relies on the integration of existing research, theories, and ideas to support arguments and provide credibility to a paper. However, it is essential to properly credit original authors whenever incorporating their work. Failing to do so, whether intentionally or unintentionally, constitutes plagiarism, which is a serious academic offense with consequences ranging from grade penalties to more severe disciplinary actions. Proper citation not only ensures academic integrity but also strengthens the credibility of your work by demonstrating engagement with established research.

There are three primary ways to incorporate sources into your writing: direct quotation, paraphrasing, and summarizing. Each method requires proper citation to acknowledge the original author.

DIRECT QUOTATION

This involves using an author's exact words and enclosing them in quotation marks. A proper citation follows immediately after to indicate the source. Direct quotations should be used sparingly, typically when the original wording is particularly impactful or precise.

> **Example of direct quotation:**
> *According to historian John Smith, "Martin Luther's 95 Theses were a pivotal moment in religious history" (Smith, 2019, p. 45).*

If you use too many direct quotations, not enough of *you* as the author of the paper is present, and your work becomes little more than a "conversation on the bus," as the reader bounces from one view to the next.

PARAPHRASING

This method involves rewriting an author's ideas in your own words while maintaining the original meaning. Paraphrasing is useful for integrating research smoothly into your writing while demonstrating comprehension of the material. Even though the wording has changed, the idea still belongs to the original author and must be cited.

Example of paraphrasing:

Martin Luther's 95 Theses significantly contributed to religious reforms in Europe, challenging the authority of the Catholic Church (Smith, 2019).

SUMMARIZING

A summary condenses the main ideas of a source, providing a broad overview rather than focusing on specific details. Like quotations and paraphrases, summaries also require citations to acknowledge the original work.

Example of summarizing:

Smith (2019) argues that the Protestant Reformation was largely influenced by Luther's writings, which questioned traditional religious authority.

Examples of Citation Formats

Different academic disciplines use various citation styles, each with its own formatting rules. The most commonly used styles include Turabian, Modern Language Association (MLA), and American Psychological Association (APA).

Chicago/Turabian Style (Footnotes and Bibliography)

The Chicago/Turabian citation style is widely used in humanities disciplines such as history, theology, and the arts. It is known for its detailed approach to citation, offering two main formats: notes and bibliography (NB) and author-date. The notes and bibliography system is the most commonly used, relying on footnotes or endnotes for in-text citations and a full bibliography at the end of the paper. This system is particularly useful for research-heavy papers that require extensive citations and references to multiple sources.

USE FOOTNOTES FOR CITATIONS

In the notes and bibliography system, citations are provided in footnotes at the bottom of the page or in endnotes at the end of the document. Each time a source is referenced, a superscript number ([1]) is placed at the end of the sentence, and the corresponding footnote contains full citation details. Footnotes provide detailed source information while keeping the main text clean and readable.

Example footnote citation:
Martin Luther's 95 Theses challenged the authority of the Catholic Church and initiated widespread religious reform.[1]

Corresponding footnote entry:
[1] John Smith, *The Protestant Reformation: A Historical Perspective* (New York: Oxford University Press, 2019), 45.

If the same source is cited multiple times, the shortened citation format can be used after the first full citation:
[2] Smith, *The Protestant Reformation*, 78.

This method helps maintain clarity and prevents unnecessary repetition while still providing proper attribution.

CREATE A BIBLIOGRAPHY

At the end of a research paper, a bibliography lists all sources used, arranged alphabetically by the author's last name. Unlike footnotes, bibliography entries are formatted slightly differently, with the author's last name listed first.

Example bibliography entry:
Smith, John. *The Protestant Reformation: A Historical Perspective*. New York: Oxford University Press, 2019.

Bibliography entries do not use superscript numbers and follow specific punctuation and formatting rules. If multiple works by the same author are listed, they should be arranged in chronological order of publication.

KEY FORMATTING RULES FOR CHICAGO/TURABIAN STYLE

- Use Times New Roman, 12-point font, and double-spacing for the main text.
- Indent footnotes and single-space within footnote entries.
- Number footnotes consecutively throughout the paper.
- The bibliography should be alphabetized and formatted with a hanging indent (where the first line is aligned left, and subsequent lines are indented).

WHY USE CHICAGO/TURABIAN STYLE?

The Chicago/Turabian style is particularly effective for research-intensive papers, allowing writers to provide thorough documentation while keeping the main text clear. It is widely used in academic writing, particularly in disciplines that emphasize source analysis and historical context. By mastering this style, you ensure that your work meets high scholarly standards while demonstrating strong research and citation practices.

Modern Language Association (MLA)

The Modern Language Association (MLA) citation style is widely used in humanities disciplines, particularly in literature, language studies, and cultural analysis. Unlike Chicago/Turabian, which relies on footnotes, MLA primarily uses in-text parenthetical citations and a *Works Cited* page at the end of the paper. This format allows for a streamlined approach to referencing sources while maintaining a clear and readable structure in academic writing.

USE IN-TEXT PARENTHETICAL CITATIONS

In MLA style, citations are placed directly in the text rather than in footnotes. A parenthetical reference includes the author's last name and the page number of the source, allowing readers to locate the full reference in the Works Cited section. This method keeps citations concise and avoids disrupting the flow of writing.

Example in-text citation:
Martin Luther's 95 Theses significantly contributed to the spread of Protestantism across Europe (Smith 45).

If the author's name is mentioned in the sentence, only the page number needs to be included in parentheses:
According to Smith, Martin Luther's 95 Theses played a crucial role in challenging the authority of the Catholic Church (45).

For sources with multiple authors, both last names should be included:
(Smith and Johnson 78).

If citing a source without an author, use the title of the work in quotation marks:
("Reformation Movements" 12).

CREATE A WORKS CITED PAGE

At the end of the paper, MLA style requires a Works Cited page that lists all sources referenced. Entries should be alphabetized by the author's last name and formatted using a hanging indent (where the first line is aligned left, and subsequent lines are indented).

Example Works Cited entry for a book:
Smith, John. *The Protestant Reformation: A Historical Perspective.* Oxford University Press, 2019.

Example Works Cited entry for a journal article:
Johnson, Emily. "Religious Reforms in 16th-Century Europe." *Historical Studies Journal*, vol. 45, no. 2, 2020, pp. 112–130.

Example Works Cited entry for an online source:
"Reformation Movements." *History of Christianity Online, 2021*, www.historyofchristianity.com/reformation-movements. Accessed 5 Jan. 2023.

Key Formatting Rules for MLA Style

- Use Times New Roman, 12-point font, and double-spacing throughout the paper.
- Indent the first line of each paragraph and use 1-inch margins on all sides.
- Italicize book titles and use quotation marks for article titles.
- Arrange the Works Cited page alphabetically by the author's last name.
- Use shortened citations when referring to the same source multiple times in a row.

First citation:
(Millard J. Erickson, *Christian Theology* 85)

Subsequent citations (same source):
(Erickson 87)

Why Use MLA Style?

MLA format is ideal for humanities disciplines because it allows for seamless integration of sources into the text while maintaining readability. It prioritizes clarity and accessibility, making it easier for readers to locate referenced works. By mastering MLA style, writers ensure that their academic work adheres to established standards, demonstrates proper research methods, and upholds ethical citation practices.

American Psychological Association (APA)

The American Psychological Association (APA) citation style is widely used in the social sciences, including psychology, education, sociology, and business. APA style emphasizes clarity, precision, and consistency in academic writing, making it particularly useful for research-based papers that require extensive citation of sources. Unlike Chicago/Turabian, which primarily uses footnotes, and MLA, which focuses on literary analysis, APA style relies on in-text citations and a *References* page to document sources.

Use In-Text Citations In APA Style

In APA format, sources are cited directly in the text using the author-date method. This allows readers to locate the full reference in the References page at the end of the document. An APA in-text citation includes the author's last name, the year of publication, and the page number (if applicable).

Example in-text citation for a direct quote:
"Martin Luther's 95 Theses significantly contributed to religious reform" (Smith, 2019, p. 45).

Example paraphrased idea:
Smith (2019) argues that Martin Luther's 95 Theses played a critical role in the Reformation.

For works with two authors, include both names:
(Smith & Johnson, 2020, p. 78).

For three or more authors, use "et al." after the first author's name:
(Brown et al., 2021).

If citing an online source without page numbers, use a paragraph number or section heading:
(Jones, 2022, para. 4) or (Jones, 2022, "Reformation Influences" section).

Create a References Page

The References page in APA style lists all sources cited in the paper. Unlike MLA's Works Cited or Chicago's Bibliography, APA references follow a distinct format that includes the author's last name, first initial, year of publication, title, and source information. References should be double-spaced and formatted with a hanging indent (where the first line is left-aligned and subsequent lines are indented).

Example book citation:
Smith, J. (2019). The Protestant Reformation: A Historical Perspective. Oxford University Press.

Example journal article citation:

Johnson, E. (2020). Religious reforms in 16th-century Europe. *Historical Studies Journal, 45*(2), 112–130. https://doi.org/xxxx.

Example online source citation:

History of Christianity Online. (2021). *Reformation movements*. Retrieved January 5, 2023, from www.history ofchristianity.com/reformation-movements.

KEY FORMATTING RULES FOR APA STYLE

- Use Times New Roman, 12-point font, and double-spacing throughout the document.
- Include a title page with the paper title, your name, institution, course name, instructor's name, and date (centered and double-spaced).
- Use 1-inch margins on all sides and an indented first line for each new paragraph.
- Use a running head (abbreviated title) and page numbers in the top-right corner of each page.
- Arrange the References page alphabetically by the author's last name.

WHY USE APA STYLE?

APA style is the preferred format in social sciences, education, and psychology because it prioritizes clarity, conciseness, and consistency. It ensures that research is properly documented, making it easy for readers to locate and verify sources. By mastering APA formatting, writers enhance the credibility of their academic work while adhering to professional and ethical research standards.

Best Practices for Notetaking

Effective notetaking is an essential skill for academic writing, as it helps you organize information, track key ideas, and ensure accurate attribution of sources. Strong note-taking habits not only improve the efficiency of your research process but also prevent accidental plagiarism, which can occur when sources are not properly documented. By implementing best practices for notetaking, you can ensure that your research remains well-structured and ethically sound.

The first step in effective notetaking is to read the source carefully and identify key ideas. Instead of copying large sections of text, focus on understanding the author's main argument, supporting evidence, and any significant conclusions. This process allows you to distinguish between major themes and minor details, helping you prioritize the most relevant information for your research.

As you take notes, it is crucial to summarize main points in your own words in a separate document or in a notebook. Paraphrasing as you write forces you to engage with the material and ensures that you do not accidentally duplicate the author's wording later. However, if you need to capture an exact phrase or statement, always mark direct quotes with quotation marks immediately to avoid confusion between your own words and those of the original author. Failing to do so can lead to unintentional plagiarism when drafting your paper.

Another critical aspect of notetaking is to record full citation details while gathering information. This includes the author's name, title of the work, publication year, page numbers, and source type (book, journal article, or website). Keeping detailed records from the beginning will save time later when compiling citations and creating your bibliography. Missing citation details can lead to difficulties in locating sources and may result in improper referencing.

To enhance organization and clarity, consider using color coding or highlighting to differentiate between direct quotes, paraphrases, and personal thoughts. For example, you might highlight direct quotes in one color, paraphrased ideas in another, and personal reflections or questions in a third one. This visual distinction helps you quickly locate specific types of information when drafting your paper, making the writing process more efficient.

By following these best practices, you will develop a systematic and reliable approach to note-taking. This will not only improve the quality of your research but also ensure that you properly credit all sources, maintain academic integrity, and produce well-supported arguments in your writing.

Apply Your Learning: Citation Exercise and Source Integration

Mastering proper citation and source integration is essential for developing a strong academic paper. Citations not only provide credibility to your arguments but also demonstrate engagement with existing research. The ability to correctly cite sources—whether through direct quotations, paraphrases, or summaries—ensures that your work maintains academic integrity while supporting your thesis with well-researched evidence. This exercise will help you practice effective citation methods and refine your ability to incorporate sources into your writing smoothly.

First, stop and take the time to create five citations from five of your ten sources. These citations may take different forms:

- *Direct quotes*—use the exact wording of the source enclosed in quotation marks.
- *Paraphrases*—rewrite an idea in your own words while maintaining its original meaning.
- *Summaries*—condense the main points of a source into a concise statement.

Ensure proper citation format based on the required style (Chicago/Turabian, MLA, or APA).

- *Chicago/Turabian*—include footnotes or endnotes with complete citation details.
- *MLA*—ensure proper in-text parenthetical references and a corresponding Works Cited entry.

- *APA*—follow the author-date method and include a properly formatted References page entry.

Second, write a short integration paragraph (four to five sentences) for each citation, explaining how it contributes to your research. Consider how the source supports your thesis, provides historical or contextual background, presents opposing viewpoints, or strengthens your argument. Clearly stating why a source is relevant will help you integrate it more effectively in your final paper.

> **Example integration paragraph:**
> *This quote highlights the pivotal role of Martin Luther's 95 Theses in initiating the Protestant Reformation. By directly confronting the Catholic Church's practices, Luther's writings sparked theological debates and inspired reforms across various European regions. This source provides historical context for my paper's argument that religious dissent played a crucial role in shaping modern Christian doctrine. Additionally, it supports my thesis by demonstrating how printed materials contributed to the rapid spread of Reformation ideas.*

Completing these exercises will help you refine your research skills and develop a stronger understanding of how to incorporate evidence into your writing. By practicing proper citation and analysis, you will be better prepared to construct a well-supported, academically sound research paper.

Final Thoughts

Understanding how to craft a strong research question and correctly cite sources is crucial to academic writing. These skills will help structure your paper and enhance your credibility as a researcher. In our next chapter, we will focus on organizing your research into an outline and structuring your thesis statement.

Happy writing!

Chapter Three

ORGANIZE YOUR PAPER

B y the end of this chapter, you will learn how to,

- Write a clear, focused thesis that presents your main argument.
- Create a structured outline to organize your ideas logically.
- Arrange your introduction, body, and conclusion for clarity and flow.

Review

Before diving into this chapter, let's take a moment to review the tasks from the last chapter. By now, you should have completed the following:

- Chosen a research topic, such as theology, history, or education.
- Collected at least ten sources related to your topic, ensuring that your research includes a mix of books, journal articles, and reputable online sources.
- Created five citations, each consisting of a tightly written paragraph summarizing the source and explaining its relevance to your research.

These tasks were designed to help you build a solid research foundation, ensuring that you have sufficient material to support your arguments as you move forward with drafting your paper. If you have not yet completed these exercises, it is important to do so as soon as possible, as they will directly impact the organization and development of your thesis and outline.

Introduction: Organize Your Paper

Now that we have explored the planning stage of writing, it's time to focus on organization—developing a strong thesis and structuring an outline. These two components serve as the backbone of your paper, ensuring clarity, coherence, and logical progression in your writing.

Why Organization Matters

Two essential components of the organizational phase are developing a strong thesis statement and structuring an outline. These elements serve as the backbone of your paper, ensuring that your ideas flow logically, your arguments remain focused, and your research is presented in a clear and effective manner. Without a well-defined thesis and an organized outline, even the strongest research can become disjointed and difficult to follow.

Effective writing isn't just about good ideas—it's about how well those ideas are structured. Each of these steps builds on previous assignments and lays the groundwork for your final paper.

Write a Strong Thesis Statement

A thesis statement is the central argument of your paper—it presents your position on a topic in a clear, concise manner. This statement acts as the foundation of your writing, guiding the structure, focus, and argument of your paper. A well-crafted thesis not only states your position but also informs the reader of the main idea and purpose of your research. Without a strong thesis, a paper can become vague or disorganized, or lack a clear direction.

A strong thesis statement should meet the following criteria:

- Takes a position on a debatable topic: Your thesis should go beyond stating a fact; it should make a claim that requires evidence and analysis.

- Offers a resolution or answers a research question: Your thesis should provide insight or a conclusion that your paper will explore in depth.

- Is tentative at first but refined throughout the writing process: As you conduct research and develop your ideas, your thesis may evolve to reflect new evidence and perspectives.

- Guides the structure and argument of your paper: Every argument and piece of evidence should support and connect back to your thesis.

Example Thesis Statements

To understand how a thesis statement shapes a paper, consider the following examples:

History paper:
"The Protestant Reformation reshaped European politics and religious structures, leading to lasting cultural transformations."—This thesis makes a historical claim and outlines specific areas of impact (politics, religion, and culture).

Education paper:
"Understanding the differences between child and adult learning theories is crucial for developing effective teaching strategies."—This statement defines a key educational debate and establishes a direction for discussion on learning strategies.

Theology paper:
"Christology in early Christian writings highlights the practical application of the atonement of Jesus."—This thesis addresses a theological issue, focusing on the concept of Christology and its complexities.

Refine Your Thesis Statement

It is important to remember that your thesis is not final—it will evolve as your research progresses. In the early stages of writing, your thesis serves as a working hypothesis that helps guide your research. As you analyze sources, develop arguments, and refine your paper's structure, be prepared to adjust, clarify, or expand your thesis to better reflect your findings.

By crafting a clear, specific, and research-driven thesis statement, you establish a strong foundation for your paper. A well-defined thesis ensures that every paragraph and argument contributes to a cohesive and compelling academic discussion.

Develop an Effective Outline

An outline is a roadmap for your paper, providing a clear structure that ensures logical flow and coherence. Creating a well-organized outline helps you visualize the overall structure of your argument, making it easier to stay on track and maintain clarity in your writing. A strong outline also prevents unnecessary repetition, helps identify weak areas in your argument, and makes the drafting process more efficient. The following steps will guide you in constructing an effective outline.

Identify Major Sections

Every research paper consists of three fundamental sections: (1) introduction, (2) body paragraphs, and (3) conclusion. These sections serve as the framework for presenting your thesis, developing your arguments, and summarizing your findings.

- *Introduction:* This section introduces your topic, provides necessary background information, and presents your thesis statement. The introduction should engage the reader and establish the purpose of your paper.
- *Body paragraphs (main arguments):* The body is where you develop and support your thesis through logical reasoning, analysis, and evidence. Each paragraph should focus on

a single main argument and be supported by relevant sources, examples, or citations.

- *Conclusion:* The conclusion summarizes your key arguments, reinforces the significance of your findings, and provides a final insight or call to action without introducing new information.

Use a Hierarchical Structure

A structured outline follows a hierarchical system, ensuring that ideas are presented in an organized manner. This system categorizes information into primary, secondary, and tertiary ideas to establish a clear flow of logic.

- *Primary ideas:* These represent your main topics or arguments. They directly support your thesis and form the basis of your body paragraphs. Each primary idea should be a strong, distinct point that contributes to your overall argument.

  Example:
  > *The role of Martin Luther's 95 Theses in the Protestant Reformation.*

- *Secondary ideas:* These provide supporting points or subtopics for each primary idea. They help expand on the argument by providing context, historical background, or theoretical perspectives.

  Example:
  > *The impact of Luther's writings on the Roman Catholic Church's authority.*

- *Tertiary ideas:* These include specific examples, evidence, or citations that substantiate your secondary ideas. This level of detail ensures that your argument is well-supported with facts, direct quotes, statistics, or scholarly interpretations.

  Example:
  > *Papal responses to the 95 Theses and the Council of Trent's reforms.*

Why Outlining Matters

Outlining is an essential step that allows you to structure your research logically, identify gaps in your argument, and streamline the drafting process. By breaking down your paper into clear sections and organizing ideas hierarchically, you create a well-structured, persuasive, and academically rigorous piece of writing. A strong outline ensures that your research paper flows logically and persuasively, and effectively communicates your thesis.

Example Outline

Topic: The Protestant Reformation

    I. Introduction

        A. Background on the Reformation

        B. Importance of religious reform

        C. Thesis statement: "The Protestant Reformation reshaped European politics and religious structures, leading to lasting cultural transformations."

    II. Theological Causes of the Reformation

        A. Corruption in the Catholic Church

        B. Martin Luther and the 95 Theses

        C. Doctrinal disputes (justification by faith)

    III. Political and Social Impact

        A. The English Reformation

        B. The Counter-Reformation

        C. Long-term effects on European governance

    IV. Conclusion

        A. Summary of main points

        B. Lasting impact of the Reformation

        C. Restating thesis in a conclusive manner

Apply Your Learning: Refine Your Thesis and Outline

Now that you have developed a preliminary thesis statement and gathered research materials, it is time to refine your argument and structure your paper effectively. A strong thesis and a well-organized outline serve as the foundation of a compelling research paper, ensuring clarity, coherence, and logical progression in your writing. This exercise will help you strengthen your thesis statement, create a structured outline, and expand your research base by incorporating additional sources.

Refine Your Thesis Statement

Your thesis statement should evolve as you conduct more research and receive feedback. If your initial thesis was too broad, consider narrowing it down to make your argument more precise. If your thesis was too vague, revise it to clearly state your position. A well-refined thesis should,

- Clearly define your central argument or research question.
- Be specific and debatable, allowing room for analysis and discussion.
- Reflect new insights gained from your research.

For example, an early thesis statement such as "The Protestant Reformation changed Europe" is too broad. A refined version might be, "The Protestant Reformation reshaped European religious and political institutions by weakening the Catholic Church's authority, increasing literacy through printed materials, and establishing Protestant belief that challenged traditional religious structures."

This refined thesis is more focused and analytical, and provides a clear roadmap for the paper's structure.

Create a Rough Outline

Once you have a clear thesis, the next step is to create a rough outline that organizes your ideas into at least three main sections. Your outline should follow a logical structure and include the following:

- *Introduction:* Provide background information, state your research question, and present your thesis.
- *Body paragraphs:* Develop your main arguments with supporting evidence. Each paragraph should focus on a single key point related to your thesis.
- *Conclusion:* Summarize your findings, restate the significance of your research, and offer final insights.

A well-organized outline helps ensure that your arguments progress logically and that your paper remains structured and focused.

Create Five Additional Citations

To strengthen your research, identify five more sources to add to your reference list. These sources should complement the five you have already submitted, helping to expand your analysis and provide additional perspectives. These citations can include,

- books that offer historical context or theoretical background,
- peer-reviewed journal articles that present scholarly arguments and evidence, or
- reputable online sources that provide primary documents, statistics, or expert insights.

For each new citation, write a brief paragraph summarizing the source and explaining how it supports your research.

Example citation (APA style):
Smith, J. (2021). *The Role of Print Media in the Protestant Reformation.* Cambridge University Press.

Summary:
This book explores how the printing press contributed to the rapid spread of Martin Luther's ideas, making religious reform more accessible to the public. It provides detailed analysis on the role of pamphlets, translated Bibles, and mass communication in shaping the Reformation's success. This source will be valuable in my research by

demonstrating how technological advancements influenced religious movements.

Final Thoughts

By refining your thesis, structuring your outline, and expanding your research base, you will be well-prepared for the next stage: writing the first draft of your paper.

A well-organized paper begins with a clear thesis and structured outline. These foundational elements will guide your writing and improve the overall coherence of your work. In the next chapter, we will dive into the writing phase, focusing on crafting well-developed paragraphs and integrating sources effectively.

Happy outlining!

Chapter Four

CRAFT EFFECTIVE PARAGRAPHS

B y the end of this chapter, you will learn how to,

- Apply the P-I-E method to write clear, well-structured paragraphs.
- Support each paragraph with evidence, citations, and analysis.
- Connect ideas logically to strengthen flow and argument cohesion.

Review

Before moving forward with this chapter, let's take a moment to review what we've already learned. Keeping up with these important steps ensures that you are building a solid foundation for your research paper, allowing each stage of the writing process to build upon the last.

By now, you should have completed the following:

1. *Ten typed citation paragraphs:* These paragraphs summarize, paraphrase, or directly quote a source, and your citations serve as the supporting evidence for your arguments, demonstrating engagement with scholarly materials and ensuring that your paper is well-researched. If you have not yet completed this step, take time to verify that each citation

is correctly formatted in the required style (Chicago, MLA, or APA) and that each paragraph clearly explains the relevance of the source to your thesis.

2. *A rough draft outline:* This draft should include at least three major points that structure your paper's main arguments. An outline helps ensure logical flow and coherence, preventing disorganization as you begin drafting. If your outline feels too broad or lacks direction, consider refining your major points and ensuring that each section directly supports your thesis.

3. *A working thesis statement:* This statement should clearly state the main argument of your paper. Your thesis should be specific, debatable, and research-driven, guiding the structure of your paper. As your research progresses, be open to refining your thesis to better reflect the evidence and insights you gather.

A well-structured thesis, a detailed outline, and properly formatted citations will make the next stage—developing strong paragraphs using the P-I-E method—much easier.

Now that we have reviewed these foundational elements, let's move forward with learning how to craft effective paragraphs that strengthen your argument and improve the overall quality of your writing.

Introduction: Craft Effective Paragraphs

With a clearly defined thesis and well-structured outline in place, the next crucial step is paragraph development. Your research and organization provide the framework, but strong, coherent paragraphs bring that framework to life. Each paragraph serves as a building block of your argument, carrying your ideas forward with clarity and purpose. Without focused and well-developed paragraphs, even a thoroughly researched paper can come across as disjointed or unclear. This chapter will guide you in shaping paragraphs that not only support your thesis but also engage your reader with logic, unity, and flow.

To help you craft clear, logical, and persuasive paragraphs, we will walk through the P-I-E method—a structured approach that ensures each paragraph is fully developed and effectively supports your thesis. The P-I-E method consists of three essential components:

- *Point*—the topic sentence that introduces the main idea of the paragraph
- *Information*—supporting details, evidence, and citations that strengthen the argument
- *Explanation*—analysis and interpretation of the information, connecting it back to the thesis

By mastering this writing technique, you will significantly improve the clarity, coherence, and persuasiveness of your writing. Well-structured paragraphs ensure that your ideas flow logically and that your arguments are fully developed, making your research paper more effective and engaging for your readers.

Let's explore each component of the P-I-E method in detail and learn how to apply it effectively in your writing.

Understand Paragraph Structure

Your research paper should be made up of multiple well-structured paragraphs, each contributing to the development of your overall argument. If your paper is ten pages long, and each page contains approximately three to four paragraphs, you will end up writing between thirty and forty paragraphs in total. This means that ensuring each paragraph is clear, coherent, and effectively developed is crucial to the success of your paper. Strong paragraph structure enhances readability, strengthens your argument, and allows your research to be presented in a logical and persuasive manner.

A paragraph is a group of related sentences that collectively develop a single main idea. Each paragraph should focus on one specific aspect of your argument rather than trying to cover multiple unrelated points. Disorganized or unfocused paragraphs can make your paper difficult to follow, weakening your overall message. To maintain clarity and structure, every paragraph must contain the three essential elements of the P-I-E format:

1. *Point (P)*—the topic sentence that introduces the main idea of the paragraph. This sentence should clearly indicate what the paragraph will discuss and how it relates to your thesis. A strong topic sentence sets the foundation for a well-developed paragraph.

2. *Information (I)*—the evidence, examples, and supporting details that substantiate the main idea. This information can come from scholarly research, historical data, direct quotes, paraphrased material, statistics, or real-world examples. Providing strong, relevant evidence strengthens your argument and demonstrates engagement with research.

3. *Explanation (E)*—the analysis and interpretation that connect the information back to your thesis. This section explains why the evidence is significant, how it supports your argument, and what conclusions can be drawn from it. Without proper explanation, evidence can appear disconnected or underdeveloped.

Example of a Well-Structured Paragraph

Here is an example of a well-structured paragraph using the P-I-E method:

> **P:** This sentence sets the stage for the supporting details that will follow. The first sentence of your paragraph should clearly introduce its main idea. This topic sentence serves as a mini-thesis statement that guides the rest of the paragraph:
>
> > *The printing press played a crucial role in the spread of Protestant ideas during the Reformation.*

I: After stating the main idea, provide specific evidence to support it. This can include facts and data, examples, expert opinions, and quotations or paraphrases from credible sources. Here, a citation strengthens the argument by adding credible support:

> *Martin Luther's 95 Theses were widely distributed across Europe within weeks of being printed, allowing his critiques of the Catholic Church to reach a broad audience. Historian John Smith notes that "the printing press transformed religious communication by enabling mass production of reformist texts" (Smith, 2019, p. 45).*

E: The final part of the paragraph explains the significance of the information and connects it back to your thesis. This analysis clarifies the relevance of the information and ties it back to the thesis statement:

> *This widespread distribution weakened the Catholic Church's control over religious doctrine and encouraged widespread theological debate. Without the printing press, Luther's ideas may not have gained the momentum needed to challenge the established church. This demonstrates how technological advancements played a key role in religious and social change.*

When you combine these three elements, a well-written paragraph looks like this:

> **(P)** *The printing press played a crucial role in the spread of Protestant ideas during the Reformation.* **(I)** *Martin Luther's 95 Theses were widely distributed across Europe within weeks of being printed, allowing his critiques of the Catholic Church to reach a broad audience. Historian John Smith notes that "the printing press transformed religious communication by enabling mass production of reformist texts" (Smith, 2019, p. 45).* **(E)** *This widespread distribution weakened the Catholic Church's control over religious doctrine and encouraged widespread theological debate. Without the printing press, Luther's ideas may not have gained the momentum needed to challenge the established church.*

This demonstrates how technological advancements played a key role in religious and social change.

Apply Your Learning: Practice the P-I-E Method

By consistently following the P-I-E structure, you can ensure that your paragraphs are organized, well-supported, and clearly connected to your thesis statement. This approach enhances the overall clarity, coherence, and persuasiveness of your writing, making your research paper more compelling and academically rigorous.

Now that you understand the importance of paragraph structure and the P-I-E method, it's time to apply these principles to your writing. Strong, well-structured paragraphs will form the foundation of your paper, ensuring that your research is presented in a logical, clear, and persuasive manner. This exercise will help you refine your ability to develop coherent, well-supported arguments while effectively integrating citations from your sources.

As you progress in writing your paper, complete the following tasks:

1. *Write six paragraphs using the P-I-E method:* Incorporate at least one citation in each paragraph. These paragraphs will contribute to the first major section of your research paper.

2. *Ensure that each paragraph includes the three key elements of the P-I-E method:*
   a. *P*—a clear topic sentence that introduces the main idea of the paragraph
   b. *I*—supporting details, including direct quotes, paraphrases, statistics, or examples from your research
   c. *E*—analysis that connects the evidence to your thesis, explaining why the information is significant and how it strengthens your argument

By completing this exercise, you will take a significant step toward drafting your research paper. These six paragraphs will form the foundation of your paper's first major section, helping you build a strong argument supported by well-integrated research. This exercise will also reinforce proper citation practices, ensuring that you maintain academic integrity and effectively support your claims.

Final Thoughts

Mastering paragraph structure is a crucial step in writing a well-organized, clear, and persuasive research paper. Each paragraph serves as a building block that develops your argument, supports your thesis, and maintains logical progression throughout your paper. By using the P-I-E method, you ensure that each paragraph is structured effectively, providing a strong point, relevant information, and insightful explanation. This approach helps prevent weak or underdeveloped paragraphs while ensuring that your writing remains focused and coherent.

As you continue working on your research paper, remember that strong paragraphs are not isolated units—they should work together to build a seamless and convincing argument. Ensuring that each paragraph connects logically to the next is just as important as structuring each paragraph internally. This is where transitional strategies come into play, helping to create a smooth flow between ideas and guiding the reader effortlessly through your discussion.

In the next chapter, we will continue refining our writing by discussing transitional strategies that enhance the flow and readability of your paper. Effective transitions help link ideas between paragraphs, making your research more engaging, cohesive, and easy to follow. Review your work carefully, ensure that each paragraph follows the P-I-E structure, and reflect on how each section contributes to your overall thesis.

Keep practicing, and happy writing!

Chapter Five

CONSIDER WORD CHOICE AND SENTENCE STRUCTURE

B y the end of this chapter, you will learn how to,

- Improve word choice to enhance clarity and precision.
- Eliminate unnecessary words that clutter your writing.
- Use different sentence structures to create fluid, engaging prose.

Review

Recall that a well-written research paper is composed of clear, organized, and well-developed paragraphs, each contributing to the overall argument and supporting the thesis statement. A paragraph consists of a group of related sentences that explore and explain one specific idea. To maintain focus and coherence, each paragraph should align with your thesis and build upon the previous sections of your paper. Understanding how to construct effective paragraphs is essential for creating a structured and persuasive argument.

To ensure that your paragraphs are fully developed, follow the P-I-E format, which consists of three essential components:

- *Point (P)*—the topic sentence that introduces the paragraph's main idea. This sentence sets the focus of the paragraph and should clearly connect to the thesis statement. A strong topic sentence helps readers understand what to expect in the following discussion.

- *Information (I)*—the supporting details, evidence, or examples that develop the point. This section should include facts, data, quotations, historical examples, or research findings that reinforce the main idea. Well-chosen evidence strengthens your argument and provides credibility to your claims.

- *Explanation (E)*—the interpretation, analysis, or discussion that connects the supporting details back to the main point and overall thesis statement. This part explains why the evidence is significant, how it supports the argument, and what conclusions can be drawn from it. Without explanation, evidence may seem disconnected or underdeveloped.

By consistently following the P-I-E format, your paragraphs will remain focused, well-supported, and logically connected to your thesis. This method ensures that your writing is clear, persuasive, and easy to follow, making it easier for readers to engage with your argument.

Mastering paragraph structure is a key step in improving the quality of your writing. With well-organized paragraphs that follow the P-I-E format, your research paper will have stronger arguments, better clarity, and improved readability. As you continue developing your paper, keep refining your paragraphs to ensure they effectively support your thesis and contribute to a cohesive and compelling discussion.

Introduction: Consider Word Choice and Sentence Structure

In this chapter, we will focus on two critical components of strong writing: word choice and sentence structure. While previous chapters discussed the importance of outlining, developing a strong thesis statement, and crafting effective paragraphs, we now shift our attention to refining individual sentences to ensure clarity, conciseness, and coherence. Even with well-structured paragraphs, unclear or overly complex sentences can weaken your argument and make your writing difficult to follow.

Effective writing relies on precise word choice and well-constructed sentences that communicate ideas clearly and efficiently. Choosing the right words enhances the impact of your arguments, while eliminating unnecessary words improves readability. Additionally, understanding different sentence types—such as simple, compound, complex, and compound-complex sentences—will help you create a varied and engaging writing style that avoids repetition and monotony.

Mastering these techniques will strengthen your writing, making your research paper more persuasive, professional, and accessible to your audience. Let's begin by exploring how word choice influences clarity and impact in academic writing.

Strategies for Eliminating Wordiness

Wordiness weakens writing by diluting the main message. A sentence is wordy if it can be shortened without loss of meaning. Below are strategies to enhance conciseness in your writing.

Eliminate Redundancies

Redundancies occur when the same idea is repeated unnecessarily. Removing extra words allows for more direct and effective communication.

Wordy:
The small puppy was tiny in size.

Concise:
The puppy was tiny.

Avoid Unnecessary Repetition

Repeating words or phrases without adding new meaning weakens writing. Writers should strive to say things once and clearly.

Wordy:
> *Our newest professor desires to help each student become a better student academically.*

Concise:
> *Our newest professor aims to help each student grow academically.*

Cut Empty or Inflated Phrases

Phrases such as "in my opinion" or "I think that" are unnecessary because it is already understood that the paper reflects your analysis.

Wordy:
> *Due to the fact that he was late, we missed the meeting.*

Concise:
> *Because he was late, we missed the meeting.*

Simplify Sentence Structure

Prefer active voice over passive voice, and reduce clauses to phrases.

Wordy:
> *A decision was made by the committee to approve the proposal.*

Concise:
> *The committee approved the proposal.*

Avoid Unnecessary Emphasis

Overusing words such as *very*, *totally*, or *really* weakens writing.

Wordy:
> *The movie was very unique.*

Concise:
> *The movie was unique.*

Since *unique* already means "one of a kind," the word *very* is unnecessary. Removing excess modifiers makes sentences stronger and more precise.

Eliminating wordiness enhances clarity, improves readability, and strengthens writing. By applying these strategies, writers can create more direct, impactful, and professional research papers. When revising, always ask, *Can this sentence be said in fewer words while retaining its meaning?* If the answer is yes, make the necessary adjustments. Effective writing is not about using more words—it is about using the right words.

Sentence Structure: Simple, Compound, and Complex Sentences

In English grammar, sentence structure refers to the arrangement of words, phrases, and clauses to form a complete sentence. There are four basic sentence structures, each serving different purposes in communication and writing. Understanding these structures helps improve clarity, coherence, and variety in writing.

1. *Simple sentences:* A simple sentence contains one independent clause, meaning it has a subject and a verb and expresses a complete thought. It may include modifiers (adjectives, adverbs, phrases) but does not contain dependent clauses.

   Example:

   S   V
   Liam reads every night before bed.

   In this example, "Liam" is the subject, "reads" is the verb, and "every night before bed" adds detail. This type of sentence is clear and direct.

2. *Compound sentences:* A compound sentence consists of two or more independent clauses joined by a coordinating conjunction (*for, and, nor, but, or, yet, so*), a semicolon, or a conjunctive adverb (*however, therefore, meanwhile, etc.*).

Example:

IC   **C**   **IC**

The sky darkened, and a storm began to form.

Here, "The sky darkened" and "a storm began to form" are both independent clauses, joined by the coordinating conjunction "and." Compound sentences help connect related ideas smoothly.

3. *Complex sentences:* A complex sentence contains one independent clause and at least one dependent (subordinate) clause. The dependent clause does not express a complete thought and must be connected to an independent clause.

    Example:

DC   **IC**

Because she studied hard, Mia passed the exam with flying colors.

In this example, "Mia passed the exam with flying colors" is an independent clause, while "Because she studied hard" is a dependent clause that adds cause-and-effect meaning. Complex sentences provide depth and relationships between ideas.

4. *Compound-complex sentences:* A compound-complex sentence includes at least two independent clauses and one or more dependent clauses. This structure allows for complex relationships between multiple ideas.

    Example:

DC   **IC**   **C**

Although the weather was cold, we went hiking, and

IC

we enjoyed the adventure.

In this example, "Although the weather was cold" is a dependent clause. "We went hiking" and "we enjoyed the adventure" are independent clauses joined by the conjunction "and." This structure is useful for expressing detailed, layered ideas while maintaining clarity.

Why Sentence Structure Matters

Sentence structure is a fundamental aspect of effective writing. The way sentences are constructed influences clarity, coherence, and engagement, shaping how readers interpret and understand ideas. A well-structured sentence ensures that information is logically presented, easy to follow, and impactful. By using a variety of sentence types, writers can create a smooth and engaging reading experience while effectively conveying their message.

- *Simple sentences* provide clarity and directness, making them ideal for stating key ideas concisely. They help ensure that readers grasp essential points without confusion. However, relying too heavily on simple sentences can make writing feel choppy or overly simplistic.

- *Compound sentences* connect related thoughts, allowing for a natural flow of ideas. They help demonstrate cause and effect, contrast, or additional information by linking two independent clauses using coordinating conjunctions (e.g., *and, but, so*). This structure is useful for making logical connections between ideas while maintaining readability.

- *Complex sentences* add depth and relationships between ideas by incorporating both independent and dependent clauses. This allows writers to show connections between causes, conditions, or explanations, making their writing more analytical and layered. When used effectively, complex sentences enhance the sophistication of arguments while maintaining logical progression.

- *Compound-complex sentences* provide the highest level of sentence variation, allowing for detailed, sophisticated writing. By combining two independent clauses and at least one dependent clause, this structure enables writers to express complex relationships and nuanced ideas. While compound-complex sentences can add richness to writing, they should be used carefully to maintain clarity.

Using a variety of sentence structures improves readability, sustains reader engagement, and enhances the flow of writing. A well-balanced mix of simple, compound, complex, and compound-complex sentences ensures that writing remains clear, dynamic, and engaging.

Writers should be mindful of sentence variety to prevent monotony and create a smooth, well-structured, and impactful piece of writing.

Avoid Run-On Sentences

A run-on sentence occurs when two or more independent clauses are joined incorrectly without proper punctuation or conjunctions. Run-on sentences can make writing confusing and difficult to read because they fail to signal where one idea ends and another begins. To maintain clarity and coherence, writers must ensure that each independent clause is properly connected.

One common type of run-on sentence is the *fused* sentence, where two independent clauses are joined with no punctuation at all.

Example (incorrect):

IC   X   IC

Air pollution poses risks to all humans it can be deadly for asthma sufferers.

In this example, two independent clauses ("Air pollution poses risks to all humans" and "it can be deadly for asthma sufferers") are placed together without a proper conjunction or punctuation mark, making the sentence grammatically incorrect.

To correct a run-on sentence, writers have several options:

1. *Use a period:* Separate the two independent clauses into two distinct sentences:

Correct:

> *Air pollution poses risks to all humans. It can be deadly*
> *for asthma sufferers.*

2. *Use a semicolon:* Connect the two clauses with a semicolon when they are closely related:

Correct:

> *Air pollution poses risks to all humans; it can be deadly*
> *for asthma sufferers.*

3. *Use a coordinating conjunction:* Insert a coordinating conjunction (*for, and, nor, but, or, yet, so*) with a comma:

Correct:

> *Air pollution poses risks to all humans, and it can be*
> *deadly for asthma sufferers.*

4. *Use a subordinating conjunction:* Turn one of the independent clauses into a dependent clause:

Correct:

> *Because air pollution poses risks to all humans, it can be*
> *deadly for asthma sufferers.*

By understanding and applying these strategies, writers can eliminate run-on sentences, making their writing clearer, more professional, and easier to follow. Proper sentence construction ensures that each idea is logically connected and effectively communicated.

Apply Your Learning: Revise for Clarity

Now that you have practiced writing six paragraphs using the P-I-E method, it's time to refine them for clarity and readability. Clear and concise writing strengthens your argument, improves flow, and ensures that your ideas are easily understood. This revision process will focus on eliminating wordiness, enhancing sentence variety, and correcting run-on sentences.

Step 1: Review and Eliminate Wordiness

Carefully read through each of your six paragraphs and identify unnecessary words, redundant phrases, and overly complex sentences. Apply strategies such as removing repetitive ideas, cutting empty phrases, and simplifying sentence structures.

Example:

> **Wordy:** *Due to the fact that air pollution is harmful, it is important that we take action in order to reduce its effects.*

> **Concise:** *Because air pollution is harmful, we must take action to reduce its effects.*

Step 2: Ensure Sentence Variety

To maintain reader engagement, ensure that your paragraphs include a mix of simple, compound, complex, and compound-complex sentences. Avoid excessive use of one type of sentence, as it may make your writing either too basic or overly complicated.

Example of sentence variety:

> **Simple:** *Climate change affects global temperatures.*

> **Compound:** *Climate change affects global temperatures, and it also contributes to extreme weather patterns.*

> **Complex:** *Because climate change affects global temperatures, many species are struggling to adapt.*

Step 3: Identify and Correct Run-On Sentences

Review your paragraphs for run-on sentences, where independent clauses are incorrectly joined. If you find any, use appropriate punctuation, conjunctions, or sentence restructuring to correct them.

Example:

> **Run-on:** *The economy is changing businesses must adapt quickly.*

Corrected: *The economy is changing, so businesses must adapt quickly.*

Final Thoughts

Although you might struggle at first to eliminate wordiness and vary your sentence type, by implementing these revision strategies you will significantly improve the clarity, readability, and professionalism of your writing. In the next chapter we will work on further developing and enhance your writing skills.

Happy structuring, and keep refining your work!

Chapter Six

REFINE YOUR WRITING

B y the end of this chapter, you will learn how to,

- Maintain consistency in point of view and use active voice for clarity.
- Apply correct spelling, punctuation, and grammar to polish your writing.
- Proofread effectively to refine accuracy, professionalism, and flow.

Review

In the last chapter we shifted our focus from paragraph structure to refining individual sentences, ensuring clarity, conciseness, and coherence. We learned the importance of choosing precise words while eliminating unnecessary ones to enhance readability. We also examined the need for different sentence structures—simple, compound, complex, and compound-complex—to create a varied and engaging writing style.

We also learned that removing redundancies, avoiding unnecessary repetition, cutting inflated phrases, and simplifying sentence structure will make your writing clear, and that replacing passive voice with active voice makes writing more direct and impactful.

Introduction: Refine Your Writing

At this stage in your writing process, you should have completed a rough draft of two-thirds of your paper, applying knowledge of word choice, sentence structure, and paragraph development. As you refine your work, it is essential to focus on the finer details of writing—person, voice, spelling, and punctuation—to ensure that your paper is clear, professional, and grammatically sound. Even well-structured arguments can lose impact if they contain inconsistent pronoun use, incorrect verb tense, or punctuation errors.

This chapter will cover key areas that contribute to polished academic writing, including,

- Choosing the appropriate person (first, second, or third-person perspective).
- Understanding active vs. passive voice and when to use each.
- Avoiding common spelling mistakes and proofreading effectively.
- Using punctuation correctly to enhance clarity and readability.
- Recognizing and correcting split infinitives and other grammatical pitfalls.

We will discuss how to refine your work effectively, ensuring that your paper meets academic standards for clarity, coherence, and correctness. By mastering these skills, you will elevate the quality of your writing, making your arguments more compelling and professional. Let's begin by examining the role of person and voice in academic writing.

Point of View: Choose the Right Person In Academic Writing

One of the fundamental aspects of academic writing is maintaining the appropriate point of view—also known as *person.* The perspective from which you write significantly impacts the clarity, professionalism, and credibility of your paper. Choosing the correct point of view ensures that your writing remains objective, formal, and aligned with academic standards.

Types of Point of View

First-Person (I, We)

The first-person perspective is used primarily in personal essays, narratives, and reflective writing. It allows the writer to express personal opinions, experiences, or interpretations directly. However, in most academic research papers, the first person is discouraged because it can make arguments appear subjective rather than evidence-based.

Example:
I believe that history provides valuable lessons.

While this sentence expresses personal belief, an academic paper benefits from a more objective tone by removing the personal pronoun.

Second-Person (You)

The second-person perspective directly addresses the reader using "you." It is common in instructional, conversational, or persuasive writing but is not appropriate for formal academic writing because it assumes the reader's actions or beliefs.

Example:
You should always cite your sources.

This sentence sounds more like a command or advice, which does not align with academic neutrality. Instead, a more formal alternative would be,

Writers should always cite their sources.

Third-Person (He, She, It, They, One, or Nouns)

The third-person perspective is the preferred choice in academic writing because it maintains objectivity, professionalism, and authority. It distances the writer from personal bias and focuses on facts, research, and logical argumentation. Third-person writing uses scholarly sources, expert opinions, and analysis rather than personal viewpoints.

> **Example:**
> *Scholars argue that history provides valuable lessons.*

This version presents the information neutrally and academically, making it more suitable for formal research papers.

Best Practice: Use Third Person In Academic Writing

Unless specifically allowed by your instructor, academic writing should primarily use third person to ensure a formal and objective tone. Avoid first and second person unless writing a personal reflection or response paper, or in a discipline that allows subjective interpretation (such as some humanities fields).

By consistently using third-person perspective, you enhance the credibility, clarity, and professionalism of your writing, making your arguments more persuasive and research-driven.

Active vs. Passive Voice

A strong academic paper relies on the effective use of active voice, as it creates clearer, more direct, and more engaging statements. The choice between active and passive voice can impact readability, clarity, and emphasis in writing. While both have their place in academic writing, understanding when to use each is essential for improving the strength and precision of your work.

Understand Voice In Writing

ACTIVE VOICE: THE SUBJECT PERFORMS THE ACTION

In active voice, the subject of the sentence carries out the action, making the sentence stronger and more concise. This structure is preferred in academic writing because it eliminates unnecessary words and enhances clarity.

S   **V**   **O**

Example: *A surge of power destroyed the pumps.*

Here, *a surge of power* is the subject, *destroyed* is the verb, and *the pumps* is the object. The sentence is direct, clear, and impactful.

PASSIVE VOICE: THE SUBJECT RECEIVES THE ACTION

In passive voice, the object of the sentence becomes the focus, while the subject is often omitted or placed at the end. This structure can make writing less engaging and more difficult to read because it adds unnecessary words and weakens the statement.

O   **S**

Example: *The pumps were destroyed by a surge of power.*

In this case, *the pumps* (the object) become the focus, while *a surge of power* (the true subject) is placed later. The passive voice softens the impact of the statement and makes it less direct.

Best Practice: Default to Active Rather Than Passive Voice

It is best to use the active voice whenever possible to ensure your writing is clear, concise, and authoritative. Reserve the passive voice for situations where the action is more important than the actor—for example, in scientific writing when the focus is on results rather than who performed the action.

Sometimes it can be justified to use the passive voice in scientific writing:

Example:
The experiment was conducted under controlled conditions.

Here, the focus is on the experiment, rather than who conducted it, making passive voice an appropriate choice.

By favoring active voice, academic writers improve readability, enhance precision, and make arguments more persuasive. Thoughtful use of passive voice, when necessary, ensures that writing remains balanced and effective.

Split Infinitives

An infinitive consists of "to" + the base form of a verb (e.g., *to think, to dance*). A split infinitive occurs when a modifier is placed between "to" and the verb. While split infinitives are common in casual speech, they should generally be avoided in formal writing.

Example:

Incorrect: *She decided to carefully balance her workload.*

Correct: *She decided to balance her workload carefully.*

Best practice: Keep "to" and the verb together whenever possible. If necessary for clarity, a split infinitive may be acceptable in some cases.

Common Punctuation Errors

Punctuation plays a crucial role in writing, ensuring clarity and readability. However, common punctuation errors can lead to confusion or misinterpretation of ideas. Understanding proper punctuation rules helps writers create polished, professional, and error-free content.

Below are some of the most frequent mistakes writers make and how to correct them.

Misuse of Commas

Commas are often misused by being placed incorrectly, omitted where necessary, or inserted unnecessarily. Misplacing commas can disrupt sentence flow and lead to grammatical errors.

No Comma Before or After "Jr." or "Sr." In Names

One common mistake occurs when commas are placed before or after "Jr." or "Sr." in a name. In formal writing, commas should not be used in this context.

Incorrect:
John Smith, Jr., wrote the article.

Correct:
John Smith Jr. wrote the article.

The correct format keeps "Jr." or "Sr." directly attached to the name without commas.

No Comma Between the Month and Year When They Appear Alone

When only the month and year are mentioned, no comma should be placed between them. However, if the day is included, a comma is necessary.

Incorrect:
June, 1987 was a historic month.

Correct:
June 1987 was a historic month.

Correct (with day included):
On June 12, 1987, President Reagan delivered a historic speech.

Use a Comma Before Coordinating Conjunctions In Compound Sentences

In compound sentences, two independent clauses (complete thoughts) are joined by a coordinating conjunction (*for, and, nor, but, or, yet, so*). A comma should be placed before the conjunction to clarify the sentence structure.

Incorrect:
The car broke down but a rescue van arrived within minutes.

Correct:
The car broke down, but a rescue van arrived within minutes.

The comma before "but" ensures that the sentence is grammatically correct and easier to read.

In summary, using commas correctly improves sentence clarity and prevents misinterpretation. Overusing or misplacing commas can confuse readers, while omitting necessary commas can make writing difficult to follow. By applying these rules, writers can ensure that their work is grammatically sound, professional, and polished.

Proper Use of Semicolons

Use a semicolon to separate two independent clauses when a coordinating conjunction is omitted.

Example:
The seminar was postponed; the professor was ill.

Use a semicolon in complex lists where items contain commas.

Example:
The conference included speakers from Paris, France; Rome, Italy; and London, England.

Quotation Marks and Punctuation

Place commas and periods inside quotation marks.

Incorrect:
"This is incorrect".

Correct:
"This is correct."

Place citation superscripts outside quotation marks.

Example:
"The Renaissance was a period of great change."[1]

Misplaced Apostrophes: Possessives vs. Contractions

Apostrophes are commonly misused in writing, particularly with contractions and possessives.

- Use apostrophes for contractions (to replace missing letters):

    it's = it is (It's raining outside.)

    you're = you are (You're going to love this book.)

- Do *not* use apostrophes for possessive pronouns:

  Incorrect:

  The company improved it's policies.

  Correct:

  The company improved its policies.

- Use apostrophes to show possession:

  The student's book (one student)

  The students' books (multiple students, multiple books)

Format for Block Quotations

- Indent block quotes 0.5 inches from the left margin.
- Single-space the quote and omit quotation marks.
- Introduce block quotes with a colon only when it follows an independent clause (complete sentence). Otherwise, introduce the blockquote with a comma or an ellipsis.

  Correct:

  The researcher concluded,

  Incorrect:

  The researcher concluded:

Common Spelling Errors to Avoid

Spelling errors can undermine the credibility and professionalism of your writing. Even strong arguments can lose impact if simple mistakes distract the reader. Some of the most frequent spelling issues arise from homophones or commonly confused words. By recognizing and correcting these errors, writers can enhance the clarity and accuracy of their work.

Homophones: Words That Sound Alike but Have Different Meanings

Homophones are words that have the same pronunciation but different spellings and meanings. These mistakes can be difficult to catch because spell-check programs may not flag them as errors.

- their / there / they're

  their = possessive pronoun (*Their house is beautiful.*)

  there = refers to a place or position (*She left her keys over there.*)

  they're = contraction of *they are* (*They're coming to the meeting.*)

- your / you're

  your = possessive pronoun (*This is your book.*)

  you're = contraction of *you are* (*You're doing a great job.*)

- its / it's

  its = possessive form of "it" (*The dog wagged its tail.*)

  it's = contraction of *it is* (*It's a sunny day.*)

Word Confusion: Similar-Looking Words with Different Meanings

Certain words are commonly confused because they look or sound similar but have different meanings.

- affect / effect

  affect = verb meaning "to influence" (*The weather will affect our plans.*)

  effect = noun meaning "the result of an action" (*The new law had a significant effect on businesses.*)

- accept / except

  accept = verb meaning "to receive or agree" (*She accepted the job offer.*)

  except = preposition meaning "to exclude" (*Everyone attended except John.*)

- compliment / complement

  compliment = a positive remark or praise (*She gave me a nice compliment on my outfit.*)

  complement = something that enhances or completes (*The wine perfectly complements the meal.*)

Avoiding common spelling errors is essential for producing polished and professional writing. These mistakes can be difficult to spot, so careful proofreading, spell-check tools, and peer review can help catch errors before submission.

By mastering the correct usage of homophones and understanding commonly confused words, writers can enhance clarity, prevent miscommunication, and build credibility in their academic and professional work.

Apply Your Learning: Analyze a Sample Paper

Proofreading is an essential skill for refining academic writing. To practice the concepts covered in this chapter, find a sample paper online to review and identify common errors that affect clarity, readability, and professionalism. This exercise will enhance your ability to detect and correct writing mistakes, ultimately improving the quality of your own work.

As you analyze the sample paper, focus on the following areas:

1. *Point of view (person):* Ensure that the paper maintains a consistent perspective. Academic writing should primarily use third person unless otherwise specified. Look for unnecessary first-person (I, we) or second-person (you) usage, and revise sentences to maintain objectivity.

2. *Active vs. passive voice:* Identify sentences where passive voice weakens clarity, and replace them with active voice whenever possible. Active voice makes writing more direct and engaging, while passive voice can make statements vague.

   Example:

   Passive: *The experiment was conducted by the students.*

   Active: *The students conducted the experiment.*

3. *Split infinitives:* Watch for instances where a word is inserted between "to" and the verb in an infinitive phrase. While

split infinitives are sometimes acceptable for clarity, they are generally best avoided in academic writing.

Example:

Incorrect: *She decided to carefully review the report.*

Correct: *She decided to review the report carefully.*

4. *Punctuation mistakes:* Check for misplaced commas, incorrect apostrophe usage, or missing periods. Pay close attention to the proper placement of commas in compound sentences, introductory phrases, and lists.

Example:

Incorrect: *The report was well written however it contained several errors.*

Correct: *The report was well written; however, it contained several errors.*

5. *Spelling errors:* Identify and correct commonly confused words, homophones, and typographical mistakes. Even minor spelling errors can weaken credibility and readability.

Example:

Incorrect: *Their going to the conference next week.*

Correct: *They're going to the conference next week.*

As you review the sample paper, mark each error and write suggested corrections based on the strategies discussed in this chapter. Consider using track changes or margin comments if editing digitally, or highlighting and annotating corrections if working with a printed copy.

By engaging in an active revision process, you will strengthen your ability to proofread and refine your own writing. Recognizing these errors in others' work will train your eye to catch them in your own papers. With consistent practice, your writing will become clearer, more precise, and more polished, ensuring that your academic work meets high professional standards.

Final Thoughts

Mastering person, voice, spelling, and punctuation is essential for producing clear and professional academic writing. By applying these techniques and thoroughly proofreading your work, you will improve both the quality and credibility of your paper.

In the next chapter, we will focus on editing your draft to ensure clarity, coherence, and a polished final product.

Happy refining!

Chapter Seven

EDIT
YOUR PAPER

B y the end of this chapter, you will learn how to,

- Use the SCOPE method to systematically edit for spelling, grammar, and punctuation.
- Apply audio proofing techniques to improve clarity, rhythm, and flow.
- Identify and revise omissions, capitalization errors, and confusing sentence structures.

Review

Before we continue, let's review what we learned in the last chapter. Even the most well-structured arguments can lose effectiveness if marred by grammatical errors, unclear pronoun usage, or punctuation mistakes. One of the core concepts covered was choosing the appropriate point of view in academic writing. Additionally, we learned about active vs. passive voice, advocating for active voice to enhance clarity and directness while acknowledging that passive voice has its place in scientific writing where the focus is on the action rather than the actor.

We discussed common grammatical pitfalls, including split infinitives, punctuation errors, and commonly confused words, as well as the need to avoid spelling errors with homophones and frequently confused words—reinforcing the importance of careful proofreading. We considered practical strategies for refining your writing, encouraging the use of tools such as Microsoft Word's grammar check, Grammarly, and peer reviews to catch errors, setting the stage for a polished final draft.

Introduction: Edit Your Paper

Effective writing is not just about drafting content; it is also about refining and improving that content through careful editing. A well-written academic paper is the result of multiple revisions, ensuring that every sentence is clear, precise, and error-free.

The art of writing is *rewriting*, and one of the most effective ways to systematically edit your work is by using the SCOPE method—a structured approach that helps writers identify and correct common mistakes. In this chapter, we will explore the SCOPE method, which focuses on five key elements of editing:

- *Spelling*—checking for typos, misused words, and commonly confused words (e.g., *their/there/they're*)
- *Capitalization*—ensuring proper use of capital letters in names, titles, and sentence beginnings
- *Omissions*—identifying missing words, phrases, or punctuation that could affect meaning
- *Punctuation*—correcting errors with commas, periods, apostrophes, and quotation marks
- *Ear (listening for clarity)*—reading the text aloud to catch awkward phrasing, unclear wording, and grammatical errors

The SCOPE Method

By following the SCOPE method, writers can effectively edit and refine their work before submitting it. In addition to this method, we will also discuss audio proofing, a powerful strategy that involves reading your writing aloud or using text-to-speech software to catch mistakes the eye might overlook. Each of these areas plays a critical role in producing polished, professional writing.

Before finalizing any academic paper, writers should carefully review each element of the SCOPE method to ensure clarity, correctness, and readability. Mastering these editing techniques will enhance the quality of writing, making arguments more persuasive and professional.

Spelling

Spelling errors can undermine the credibility of a paper. While spell check software is useful, it does not catch every mistake, especially homophones (e.g., *their*, *there*, and *they're*). Some strategies for checking spelling include the following:

- Assume at least five words are misspelled, and search for them actively.
- Mark any words that seem ambiguous, and verify them in a dictionary.
- Have someone else review the paper for spelling mistakes.
- Do not assume a word is correct—always confirm.
- Be aware that technical terms or specialized vocabulary may not be recognized by spell checkers; manually verify them.

Capitalization

Proper capitalization is essential for maintaining clarity, professionalism, and correctness in academic writing. Incorrect capitalization can make a paper appear careless or inconsistent, while proper usage ensures that names, titles, and significant terms are given the respect and accuracy they deserve. Understanding the basic rules of capitalization helps writers avoid common errors and produce polished, professional documents.

COMMON CAPITALIZATION MISTAKES

Writers frequently make capitalization errors in the following areas:

- *Not capitalizing proper nouns:* Proper nouns refer to specific names of people, places, and organizations. These should always be capitalized.

  Incorrect:

  shakespeare was a famous playwright.

  Correct:

  Shakespeare was a famous playwright.

  Incorrect:

  First baptist church hosts community events.

  Correct:

  First Baptist Church hosts community events.

- *Incorrectly capitalizing common nouns:* Common nouns, such as *president, university,* or *church,* should only be capitalized when referring to a specific entity.

  Incorrect:

  The President will visit next week. (Not capitalized if not referring to a specific president.)

  Correct:

  President Lincoln delivered the Gettysburg Address.

- *Failing to capitalize religious terms properly:* Religious terms, including sacred texts and references to God, must be capitalized.

  Incorrect:

  The bible contains many historical accounts.

  Correct:

  The Bible contains many historical accounts.

  Incorrect:

  Faith and christianity have influenced history greatly.

  Correct:

  Faith and Christianity have influenced history greatly.

STRATEGIES FOR CHECKING CAPITALIZATION

To ensure correct capitalization, writers should,

- *Capitalize the first word of every sentence:* This basic rule prevents common mistakes in formal writing.
- *Verify that all proper nouns are capitalized:* When mentioning specific people, places, books, or organizations, ensure their names are correctly formatted.
- *Use online grammar tools:* Tools like Grammarly or Microsoft Word's spelling and grammar check can flag capitalization errors.
- *Check underlined words in Microsoft Word:* If a word is underlined in green, right click on it to see suggested corrections.

Proper capitalization enhances the readability, accuracy, and credibility of writing. By following basic capitalization rules and using editing tools to catch errors, writers can ensure that their work appears polished and professional. Careful attention to capitalization reflects attention to detail, making a strong impression on readers and instructors alike.

Omissions

Omissions refer to missing words that can disrupt the meaning and flow of a sentence. These are often harder to catch because the writer's brain fills in the gaps automatically.

STRATEGIES FOR IDENTIFYING OMISSIONS

One of the most common yet overlooked writing errors is omission, where words, phrases, or necessary punctuation marks are unintentionally left out. Omissions can make sentences confusing, incomplete, or grammatically incorrect, disrupting the flow and clarity of a paper.

Identifying and correcting omissions is a critical step in the editing process. Below are several effective strategies to help writers detect and fix missing elements in their work.

1. *Read the paper aloud slowly:* Reading your work aloud and at a slow pace forces you to engage with each word, making it easier to catch missing words or incomplete thoughts. Often, when reading silently, the brain automatically fills in missing words, making errors difficult to detect. By vocalizing each sentence, you can identify gaps in meaning and awkward sentence structures that need revision.

2. *Ask a peer to review your paper:* A fresh set of eyes can be invaluable in spotting omissions. Asking a peer, classmate, or mentor to read your paper allows them the opportunity to identify missing words, unclear transitions, or incomplete sentences that you might have overlooked. Peer reviewers can also ask clarifying questions, helping you refine areas where ideas are underdeveloped or ambiguous.

3. *Use text-to-speech software:* Hearing your paper read aloud by text-to-speech software is another effective way to detect missing words and awkward phrasing. When the computer reads the text aloud, it follows exactly what is written, rather than what you expect to see. This makes omissions stand out more clearly. Many word processors, including Microsoft Word and Google Docs, offer built-in text-to-speech functions that can assist with this process.

4. *Print out the document and read it on paper:* Editing a document on a printed page rather than on a screen can make omissions easier to spot. The change in format helps the brain process the text differently, revealing errors that may have gone unnoticed during a digital review. Using a pen or highlighter, writers can mark incomplete sentences, missing punctuation, or missing transition words, ensuring that no critical elements are left out.

Omissions can weaken clarity and disrupt the logical flow of a paper. By using multiple editing techniques, such as reading aloud, peer review, text-to-speech tools, and printed copies, writers can identify and correct missing words or phrases effectively. Careful editing ensures that ideas are fully developed, grammatically complete, and clearly presented, leading to a stronger, more polished academic paper.

Punctuation

Punctuation plays a crucial role in clarity, readability, and meaning in writing. Misplaced or missing punctuation can lead to misunderstandings, ambiguity, and a lack of professionalism. While punctuation may seem like a minor detail, it significantly impacts how a reader interprets a sentence. Below are some common punctuation errors and strategies for ensuring correct usage.

MISPLACED COMMAS IN COMPOUND SENTENCES

A common mistake is omitting or misplacing commas in compound sentences. When two independent clauses are joined by a coordinating conjunction (*for, and, nor, but, or, yet, so*), a comma must precede the conjunction.

Incorrect:
> *The professor lectured for two hours but the students remained attentive.*

Correct:
> *The professor lectured for two hours, but the students remained attentive.*

INCORRECT USAGE OF SEMICOLONS AND COLONS

Many writers struggle with when to use semicolons and colons. Semicolons connect two closely related independent clauses without a coordinating conjunction.

Correct:
> *The semester is ending; final exams start next week.*

Colons introduce lists, explanations, or quotations, and what follows does not need to be an independent clause.

Correct:
> *Three factors contributed to the decision: budget constraints, time limitations, and available resources.*

Using these punctuation marks incorrectly or interchangeably can lead to reader confusion.

FORGETTING QUOTATION MARKS AROUND DIRECT QUOTES

Direct quotes require quotation marks to signal borrowed language. Forgetting to place quotation marks can lead to plagiarism or misrepresentation of sources.

Incorrect:

According to Smith 2020, academic success is linked to effective study habits.

Correct:

According to Smith (2020), "academic success is linked to effective study habits."

Additionally, punctuation should be placed inside quotation marks in American English.

Correct:

She said, "This is the best book I've read this year."

OVERUSE OF EXCLAMATION POINTS

While exclamation points convey emotion and excitement, they are generally inappropriate in academic writing. Excessive use makes writing appear informal or exaggerated.

Incorrect:

The research findings were incredible! They changed everything we knew about the topic!

Correct:

The research findings were significant and provided new insights into the topic.

To ensure correct punctuation, writers should review comma rules, particularly in compound and complex sentences, to avoid run-on sentences or unnecessary pauses. They should verify that all quoted material has proper quotation marks and that citations are correctly formatted.

Additionally, it is wise to consult a style guide such as APA, Turabian, or MLA to check punctuation rules and formatting guidelines, and ensure that periods and commas are placed inside quotation marks in American English. Check with your instructor first to see if there is a required style guide for your particular assignment.

Proper punctuation is essential for clear and professional writing. By understanding common punctuation errors and using careful editing techniques, writers can enhance the readability, accuracy, and credibility of their work. Paying close attention to punctuation rules ensures that academic writing is polished and effective, making it easier for readers to engage with and understand the content.

Ear (Listen for Clarity and Flow)

One of the most effective yet often overlooked editing techniques is listening to your writing aloud. Hearing a paper read aloud engages the brain differently than silent reading, making it easier to identify awkward phrasing, redundancy, missing words, and unclear ideas. The way a sentence sounds can reveal issues that are difficult to notice visually, such as run-on sentences, abrupt transitions, or confusing wording. By incorporating audio proofing, writers can refine their work for better clarity, coherence, and natural flow.

Some strategies for audio proofing are as follows:

1. *Use text-to-speech software:* Many computers, tablets, and word processing programs offer built-in text-to-speech functions that can read your document aloud. Hearing your work from an automated voice removes biases in reading, allowing you to focus on how your words actually sound rather than how you expect them to sound. If a sentence sounds awkward or confusing, it likely needs revision.

2. *Read the paper aloud to yourself or a peer:* Reading aloud forces you to engage with every word and pay closer attention to sentence structure, word choice, and clarity. If a sentence is difficult to say smoothly, it may be overly complicated or wordy. Asking a peer to listen while you read aloud can also

provide useful feedback on whether ideas flow logically and make sense to an audience.

3. *Record yourself reading the paper:* Recording yourself reading your paper allows you to listen critically and objectively. When you listen back, pay attention to,

   » sentences that sound unnatural or overly complex,
   » repetitive phrases or redundant words, or
   » missing words that disrupt meaning.

   This method allows you to pause and revise sections that do not sound clear.

4. *Pay attention to sentence rhythm and clarity:* Good writing has a natural rhythm and flow. If your sentences feel choppy or disjointed, consider combining ideas for better cohesion. If sentences seem too long or difficult to follow, consider breaking them up for readability.

Listening helps ensure that your writing sounds smooth, logical, and professional. Using your ear as an editing tool is a valuable way to enhance clarity and readability. Whether through text-to-speech software, reading aloud, recording yourself, or working with a peer, audio proofing helps catch errors that may be missed in silent reading. This final step ensures that your academic writing is polished, well-structured, and easy to understand for your audience.

Apply the SCOPE Method

To refine a paper and ensure clarity, accuracy, and professionalism, writers should apply the SCOPE method in a systematic, step-by-step approach. Instead of trying to catch every mistake at once, breaking the editing process into multiple rounds allows for focused attention on different elements of writing.

The following steps provide an effective way to implement the SCOPE method, ensuring that all aspects of a paper are thoroughly reviewed before final submission.

First Round: Review Spelling and Capitalization

Begin by carefully reviewing spelling and capitalization throughout the paper.

1. Look for common spelling mistakes, such as homophones (their/there/they're) or frequently confused words (affect/effect).

2. Ensure that proper nouns, titles, and religious terms are capitalized correctly (First Baptist Church, President Lincoln, the Bible).

Many word processors include spell-check tools, but manual review is essential since automated tools may not catch context-based errors.

Second Round: Check for Omissions and Punctuation Mistakes

Next, scan the paper for omitted words, phrases, or punctuation that could affect clarity. Missing words can lead to incomplete sentences, while omitted punctuation may create run-on sentences or confusion. Focus on,

- comma usage in compound and complex sentences,
- proper placement of quotation marks around direct quotes,
- correct semicolon and colon use in lists or explanations, and
- apostrophes in contractions and possessives (it's vs. its, student's vs. students').

Reading each sentence slowly and carefully can help detect missing words or punctuation errors that might be overlooked in a quick review.

Third Round: Read the Paper Aloud or Listen Using Text-to-Speech Software

After reviewing spelling, capitalization, omissions, and punctuation, move to listening for clarity and flow. Read the paper aloud to yourself or to a peer, or listen to it using text-to-speech software. Listening to the writing reveals awkward phrasing, redundancy, or unclear ideas that may not be noticeable through silent reading. If a sentence sounds unnatural or confusing, consider restructuring or simplifying it for better readability.

Final Round: Make Necessary Revisions

In the final round, apply all necessary revisions based on errors identified in the previous rounds. Ensure that,

- sentences are clear, concise, and well-structured,
- word choice is precise and appropriate for academic writing, and
- there is a logical flow between paragraphs and ideas are effectively connected.

This last review ensures that the paper is fully polished and free from distractions, allowing the argument to stand out clearly and persuasively.

Proofreading Strategies

Effective proofreading is an essential step in the writing process, helping to eliminate errors in spelling, punctuation, and grammar. Even well-structured papers can be weakened by minor mistakes, which can distract readers and reduce the credibility of your work. By carefully reviewing your writing, you ensure that your ideas are communicated clearly and professionally. Below are several effective proofreading strategies and tools that can enhance the quality of your writing.

Microsoft Word's Spelling & Grammar Check

One of the most accessible proofreading tools is Microsoft Word's built-in spelling and grammar check feature. This tool can help identify basic spelling errors, incorrect verb tense, and punctuation mistakes. However, while useful, it is *not* foolproof—

it may overlook homophones (e.g., *their* vs. *there*) or misinterpret certain sentence structures. Therefore, it should be used alongside manual proofreading.

Grammarly—Free and Premium Versions

For a more advanced grammar check, Grammarly provides real-time feedback on spelling, sentence structure, word choice, and clarity. The free version corrects basic errors, while the premium version offers deeper insights into style, conciseness, and academic tone. Grammarly is particularly helpful for detecting complex grammar issues and improving sentence readability. However, writers should not rely solely on AI-based tools—it is essential to review suggestions carefully to ensure they align with the intended meaning.

Read Aloud

A simple yet powerful proofreading technique is reading your work aloud. This method helps identify awkward phrasing, missing words, and run-on sentences that may be overlooked when reading silently. When spoken, errors become more noticeable, allowing you to improve sentence flow and readability. Additionally, hearing your writing read aloud helps ensure clarity and a natural tone.

Peer Review

Asking a classmate, colleague, or mentor to review your work provides fresh insight. Another reader may catch errors, unclear arguments, or inconsistencies that you might have missed. Peer feedback is especially valuable for improving structure, coherence, and logical flow. To maximize effectiveness, provide your reviewer with specific areas of focus, such as grammar, sentence clarity, or argument development.

Proofreading is a crucial step in producing a polished, professional research paper. Using a combination of automated tools, self-review techniques, and peer feedback helps your writing is error-free and well-structured. While technology can assist in identifying mistakes, nothing replaces a careful, detailed review by the writer. By incorporating these strategies, you will enhance the accuracy, clarity, and overall impact of your writing.

Final Thoughts

By following these four rounds of revisions, writers can effectively apply the SCOPE method to produce error-free, well-organized, and professional writing. Dividing the editing process into separate stages allows for thorough proofreading, preventing overlooked mistakes and ensuring that the final draft is cohesive, polished, and ready for submission.

By now, your paper should be fully drafted. The next step is refining it through rigorous editing. Use the strategies discussed in this chapter to make necessary corrections and finalize your work. Never submit the first draft. Editing and proofreading are crucial to producing high-quality academic writing. Take the time to review your work carefully.

Happy editing!

Chapter Eight

FINALIZE YOUR PAPER

B y the end of this chapter, you will learn how to,

- Conduct a final review to ensure clarity, coherence, and proper formatting.
- Write engaging introductions and strong conclusions that frame your argument.
- Prepare and polish your paper for professional, submission-ready presentation.

Review

Our last chapter emphasized the importance of refining and improving writing through careful editing and proofreading. A well-written academic paper results from multiple revisions, making sure every sentence is error free and communicates ideas effectively. We were introduced to the SCOPE method, a structured approach to editing that helps writers identify and correct common mistakes by focusing on five key areas of editing: spelling, capitalization, omissions, punctuation, and ear (listening for clarity). We discussed how breaking the editing process into multiple rounds ensures thorough proofreading. By systematically applying the SCOPE method, writers can refine their work to produce polished, professional, and error-free academic papers.

Editing is not just about fixing mistakes; it is about enhancing readability, ensuring logical flow, and strengthening arguments. Taking the time to review and revise writing thoroughly ensures that the final paper is clear, persuasive, and ready for submission.

Introduction: Finalize Your Paper

In this chapter, we will focus on how to finalize your paper to meet academic standards. By reading your paper as an instructor would, you can ensure clarity, coherence, and correctness.

Additionally, we will focus on crafting strong introductory and concluding paragraphs, finalizing according to your formatting style, and preparing your paper for submission.

Review Your Paper

Now that your paper is near completion, it's time to conduct a final, thorough review before submission. This revision should focus on the following:

- *Ensuring logical flow and coherence:* Does each paragraph connect with the previous paragraph smoothly? Are your arguments presented in a logical order?

- *Eliminating redundancy:* Remove any repetitive words or unnecessary phrases that do not contribute to your argument.

- *Checking formatting consistency:* Ensure that your paper follows the required academic style guide (APA, MLA, or Turabian) for citations, headings, and references.

- *Verifying citation accuracy:* Double check that all sources are correctly cited and formatted according to your instructor's requirements.

This final review ensures that your paper is error free, clearly structured, and professionally presented. By applying the SCOPE method and conducting a comprehensive review, you can confidently submit a well-polished and compelling academic paper.

If time allows, take a short break before the final review. Returning to your writing with a fresh perspective will help you catch additional errors and refine your work even further.

Write the Introduction and Conclusion

Your introduction and conclusion serve as the bookends of your paper, framing your argument and reinforcing your key points. A well-written introduction sets the stage for your discussion, while a strong conclusion leaves a lasting impression on the reader. Often, these sections are best written after completing the body of your paper. This allows you to clearly define your thesis in the introduction and reinforce your findings in the conclusion based on the content you have developed.

Write an Effective Introduction

A compelling introduction is concise, engaging, and informative, providing the reader with a clear understanding of your paper's purpose. For a standard academic paper, an introduction should typically be 50–150 words and include three to five sentences that establish your argument.

Key components of an introduction include,

- *An engaging opening sentence:* Start with an attention-grabbing statement that introduces the topic and highlights its significance. Avoid generic or vague openings.

  Example:
  Throughout history, technological advancements have transformed the way humans communicate, shaping cultures and economies alike.

- *A clear thesis statement:* Your thesis is the central argument or focus of your paper. It should be specific and debatable, and provide a roadmap for your discussion.

  Example:

  This paper argues that social media has significantly altered interpersonal communication by increasing connectivity, reshaping language, and influencing mental health.

- *A brief overview of main points:* Provide a succinct preview of the key arguments or themes you will explore in the body of your paper. However, avoid excessive background information—save that for the main sections.

  Example:

  The discussion will examine how social media affects relationships, influences language, and contributes to mental health challenges.

A well-crafted introduction engages the reader, introduces the thesis, and outlines the paper's direction without unnecessary detail.

Write an Effective Conclusion

Your conclusion serves as the final thought your reader will take away from your paper. It should reinforce your thesis, summarize key points, and leave a strong impression, without introducing new information.

Key components of a conclusion include (or do not include) the following:

- *Include a restatement of your main argument:* Reiterate your thesis without repeating it verbatim. Instead, rephrase it in a way that reinforces your central claim.

  Example:

  While social media has improved global communication, it has also transformed the way people interact, presenting both opportunities and challenges.

- *Avoid new ideas or evidence:* The conclusion is not the place to introduce new theories, statistics, or arguments. Instead, focus on summarizing and synthesizing the key findings of your paper.

- *Use an effective closing strategy:* A strong conclusion should provide a sense of closure while leaving a thought-provoking final impression. Consider one of the following strategies:

  » *Connecting back to an example or image from the introduction:* If the introduction discussed the rise of instant messaging, the conclusion could reflect on its future impact.

  » *Providing a concise summary of key findings:*

    Example:
    The analysis of social media's effects on relationships, language, and mental health highlights both its transformative power and potential risks.

  » *Ending with a thought-provoking statement:*

    As digital communication continues to evolve, society must consider how to balance innovation with meaningful human connection.

A well-crafted conclusion reinforces your thesis and ensures that your argument resonates with the reader, leaving them with a clear, impactful, and relevant final thought. Strong introductions and conclusions frame your argument effectively, guiding the reader through your ideas from start to finish. Writing them after completing the body of your paper allows you to align them seamlessly with your discussion.

By following these guidelines, you can ensure that your introduction captures interest and sets the stage, while your conclusion reinforces your argument and leaves a lasting impression.

Final Thoughts

By now you have learned essential academic writing skills that will serve as a foundation for your future research and written communication. From the initial stages of planning and organizing your research to the final steps of editing and revising, you now have the tools necessary to produce well-structured, clear, and compelling academic papers.

You have learned how to,

- Plan your research effectively by selecting appropriate topics, forming strong research questions, and gathering credible sources.

- Organize ideas into structured arguments, ensuring logical flow and coherence in your writing.

- Write clear and coherent paragraphs using the P-I-E method (point, information, explanation).

- Edit and proofread professionally by applying strategies such as the SCOPE method and audio proofing to refine your work.

- Revise for clarity and academic integrity, ensuring proper citation, avoiding plagiarism, and presenting ideas with precision.

Now, all that remains is for you to write your paper. Remember that the art of writing is *rewriting*. Take time for a final review, ensuring that your writing reflects your best effort and academic growth.

Happy writing!

APPENDIX: LEARNING HANDOUTS

P.O.W.E.R. Up! Citation Worksheet -Refining Your Research-

Citations are essential for academic integrity and proper research documentation. They serve to give credit to original authors, provide evidence to support arguments, and prevent plagiarism.

There are three primary ways to incorporate sources:

1. *Direct quotation*—using an author's exact words enclosed in quotation marks.

2. *Paraphrasing*—rewriting an author's ideas in your own words while maintaining the original meaning.

3. *Summarizing*—condensing the main points of a source in a broad overview.

Part 1: Practice Identifying Research Questions

A strong research question should be:

- *Clear and specific*—focused on a particular issue.
- *Researchable*—answerable using credible sources.
- *Balanced in scope*—neither too broad nor too narrow.
- *Analytical*—encourages discussion and critical thinking.

Exercise

Evaluate the following research questions and determine if they are clear, researchable, balanced, and analytical. Suggest improvements where necessary.

1. What causes pollution?

2. How does social media influence political opinions among college students?

3. Is technology good or bad?

4. How did the printing press contribute to the spread of the Reformation?

Part 2: Citation Style Identification

Different academic disciplines use various citation styles. The three most common are,

1. **MLA (Modern Language Association)**—used in humanities and literature.

2. **APA (American Psychological Association)**—used in social sciences and education.

3. **Chicago/Turabian**—used in history, theology, and some social sciences.

Exercise

Match the following disciplines with their preferred citation style:

1. Psychology

2. Literature

3. History

4. Business

5. Philosophy

6. Sociology

Part 3: Citation Formatting Practice

Exercise

Format the following source information in MLA, APA, and Chicago styles:

Author: Jane Smith

Title: *The Evolution of Technology*

Publisher: Oxford University Press

Year: 2021

Page: 45

Write the citation in each style below:

MLA:

APA:

Chicago:

Part 4: Citation Integration Exercise

Using the following sentence, incorporate a citation in MLA, APA, and Chicago styles:

> *The Industrial Revolution drastically changed the workforce, leading to urbanization and technological advancements.*

Rewrite the sentence with an appropriate citation in each style:

MLA:

APA:

Chicago:

Part 5: Avoiding Plagiarism

Plagiarism occurs when sources are not properly credited. This includes copying text without citation, incorrect paraphrasing, and failing to include quotation marks for direct quotes.

Exercise

Identify whether the following statements are examples of plagiarism. Mark "P" for *plagiarism* and "C" for *correctly cited*:

_____ *According to Smith (2021), "The Industrial Revolution drastically changed the workforce."*

_____ *The Industrial Revolution led to urbanization and technological advancements.*

_____ *Smith argues that the Industrial Revolution was a turning point in global history (Smith, 2021).*

_____ *"The Industrial Revolution was a turning point" (Smith, 2021, p. 45).*

Part 6: Citation Application Activity

Exercise

Find five sources related to your research topic. For each source, create a citation in the style required for your academic discipline (MLA, APA, or Chicago). Then, write a short paragraph explaining how the source contributes to your research.

> **Example:**
>
> **Citation (MLA):** Smith, John. *The History of Industrialization.* Oxford University Press, 2021.
>
> **Integration paragraph:** *This book provides a comprehensive history of industrialization and its effects on society. It supports my research by offering background information on economic and technological changes during the Industrial Revolution.*

Source 1:

Citation:

Integration paragraph:

Source 2:

Citation:

Integration paragraph:

Source 3:

Citation:

Integration paragraph:

Source 4:

Citation:

Integration paragraph:

Source 5:

Citation:

Integration paragraph:

Final Reflection

After completing this worksheet, reflect on the following questions:

1. What are the key differences between MLA, APA, and Chicago citation styles?

2. Why is proper citation crucial in academic writing?

3. How will you ensure you properly integrate sources in your research paper?

By mastering citations and research question formation, you strengthen your ability to conduct thorough, ethical, and credible academic research.

P.O.W.E.R. Up! Exercise
-Outlining a Paper-

Introduction

An outline is a structured way to organize your ideas before writing a paper. A well-constructed outline ensures that your paper has a clear introduction, logical body points, and a strong conclusion. This exercise will guide you through creating an outline for a paper with an introduction, main points, and a conclusion.

Instructions

1. Choose a research topic.

2. Develop a strong thesis statement.

3. Identify three main points that support your thesis.

4. Add supporting evidence or examples for each point.

5. Write a conclusion summarizing the key arguments and restating the thesis.

Example Outline

Topic: The Impact of Social Media on Society

    I. Introduction

        A. Brief background on social media growth

        B. Importance of studying its impact

        C. Thesis statement: Social media has significantly influenced communication, mental health, and political engagement.

II. Body paragraphs

    A. Influence on communication

        1. Instant connectivity and global reach

        2. Decline in face-to-face interactions

    B. Effects on mental health

        1. Increased anxiety and depression due to comparison culture

        2. Positive effects: support communities and mental health awareness

    C. Role in political engagement

        1. Social media as a tool for political campaigns

        2. Spread of misinformation and echo chambers

III. Conclusion

    A. Summary of key points

    B. Restate thesis in a conclusive way

    C. Call to action or final thought on responsible social media use

Apply Your Learning

Now, create an outline for your own research paper using the structure above. Be sure to,

1. develop a strong thesis statement,

2. identify three key supporting points,

3. provide evidence or examples for each point, and

4. conclude with a summary and restatement of your thesis.

Thesis Statement:

I.

II.

III.

Summary and Restatement of Thesis:

P.O.W.E.R. Up! Exercise
-Writing a Paragraph In P-I-E Format-

A well-structured paragraph should follow the P-I-E format: point, illustration, and explanation. This method ensures clarity, coherence, and logical flow in writing.

P-I-E Format

1. *Point (P)*—the main idea or argument of the paragraph. This should be a clear and concise topic sentence that sets up what the paragraph will discuss.

2. *Illustration (I)*—provides evidence, examples, or data to support the main point. This can include direct quotes, statistics, or real-world examples.

3. *Explanation (E)*—connects the evidence to the point by explaining why the illustration is significant and how it supports the topic sentence.

Example of a P-I-E Paragraph

Topic: The Importance of Reading in Academic Success

Point: Reading regularly enhances students' academic performance by improving comprehension skills and critical thinking.

Illustration: According to a study by the National Literacy Institute (2020), students who engage in daily reading score 20% higher on standardized tests compared to those who do not.

Explanation: This data shows that regular reading significantly impacts students' ability to process and understand complex information, which is essential for academic success.

Exercise: Write Your Own P-I-E Paragraph

Choose one of the following topics and write a paragraph following the P-I-E format. Ensure that your paragraph includes a clear point, a strong illustration, and an effective explanation.

Topics:

1. The benefits of exercise on mental health

2. The role of technology in modern education

3. The impact of social media on communication

P.O.W.E.R. Up! Exercise
-Eliminating Wordiness-

Introduction

Effective writing requires clarity and conciseness. Wordiness weakens writing by diluting the main message and making sentences unnecessarily long. This exercise will help you recognize and eliminate wordiness to improve readability and strengthen your writing.

Strategies for Eliminating Wordiness

1. *Eliminate Redundancies*
   Redundant words and phrases repeat the same idea unnecessarily. Removing extra words makes sentences more direct.

   Example:

   Wordy: *The small puppy was tiny in size.*

   Concise: *The puppy was tiny.*

2. *Avoid Unnecessary Repetition*
   Repeating words or phrases without adding new meaning weakens writing. Say things once and clearly.

   Example:

   Wordy: *Our professor wants each student to become a better student.*

   Concise: *Our professor wants each student to improve.*

3. *Cut Empty or Inflated Phrases*
   Some phrases add no real meaning to a sentence. Removing them makes writing more precise.

Example:

Wordy: Due to the fact that he was late, we missed the meeting.

Concise: Because he was late, we missed the meeting.

4. *Simplify Sentence Structure*

Prefer active voice over passive voice, and reduce unnecessary clauses.

Example:

Wordy: A decision was made by the committee to approve the proposal.

Concise: The committee approved the proposal.

5. *Avoid Unnecessary Emphasis*

Words such as *very, totally,* or *really* often weaken writing.

Example:

Wordy: The movie was very unique.

Concise: The movie was unique.

Exercise: Eliminate Wordiness

Revise the following sentences to eliminate wordiness while retaining the original meaning:

1. At this point in time, we are currently reviewing the new proposal.

2. The reason why I left the meeting early was because I had another appointment.

3. There is a need for additional research in the area of climate change studies.

4. In my personal opinion, I think that the policy should be revised.

5. The fact that she is an expert in the field means that her advice is valuable.

Final Thoughts

Eliminating wordiness enhances clarity and professionalism in writing. As you revise your work, ask yourself, *Can this sentence be said in fewer words while retaining its meaning?* If the answer is yes, make the necessary adjustments.

Strong writing is about using the right words—not more words.

P.O.W.E.R. Up! Editing Exercise -MLA Format Writing Sample-

John Doe

Professor Smith

ENG101 - English Composition

October 12 2023

the effects of technology on education

Technology has had a huge impact on education in the 21st century. It is important to understand how it effects learning. Many students use laptops, tablets, and even smartphones in class, but some teachers think this is distracting. on the other hand, some studies show that digital tools can actually improve learning outcomes (Johnson, 2018). In this essay, I will discuss how technology has improved education and why it should be used more often.

First of all, technology makes education more accessible. For example, online courses allow students to learn at their own pace. Many people who have jobs or families can get a degree online. Additionally, digital tools help students with disabilities access learning materials (smith 2019). Another benefit of technology is that it makes learning more interactive. Instead of just reading textbooks, students can watch videos and use educational apps to help understand difficult concepts.

However, there are some disadvantages. Some people argue that using too much technology reduces critical thinking skills. If students rely on Google for all their answers, they may not learn how to analyze information. Additionally, not all schools have the same access to technology, which can create inequality between students. But overall, technology has more benefits than disadvantages in education.

To conclude, technology has changed education in many ways. While there are some drawbacks, it is mostly beneficial. schools should use more technology to improve learning. As technology continues to evolve, it will be even more important in the classroom.

Works cited

Johnson, Mark. "The Digital Classroom: How Technology is Transforming Education." New York: Academic Press, 2018.

Smith, Laura. Education in the Digital Age. Chicago: Learning Press 2019

Editing Questions

1. Identify three grammar mistakes in the essay.

2. Find at least two MLA formatting errors in the Works Cited section.

3. Locate an in-text citation mistake and correct it.

4. Identify one sentence that lacks clarity, and suggest an improvement.

5. Find at least one capitalization or punctuation mistake.

Answer Key

1. *Grammar mistakes:* "effects" should be "affects"; "on the other hand" should start a new sentence; "schools" should be capitalized in the conclusion.

2. *MLA formatting errors:* "Works cited" should be "Works Cited"; book titles should be italicized; entries should be in alphabetical order and have proper indentations.

3. *In-text citation mistake:* "(smith 2019)" should be "(Smith 2019)."

4. *Clarity issue:* "schools should use more technology to improve learning" is vague; it should be specific—e.g., "Public schools should integrate more digital tools into their curriculum to enhance student engagement."

5. *Capitalization and punctuation:* "the effects of technology on education" should be capitalized properly as "The Effects of Technology on Education"; missing period in Works Cited after "Learning Press 2019".

P.O.W.E.R. Up! SCOPE Editing Process

Introduction

The SCOPE editing process is a structured method to help you revise and improve your writing. By focusing on five key aspects, you can refine your papers to enhance readability, coherence, and academic integrity.

SCOPE Editing Process

The SCOPE editing process is a systematic approach to reviewing and refining writing. Each letter in SCOPE represents an essential element of editing: spelling, capitalization, omissions, punctuation, and ear (listening for clarity and flow). Use this handout as a guide to improve the quality of your writing.

Spelling

1. Check for misspelled words using a spell checker, but also manually review for words that may be correctly spelled but misused (e.g., their/there/they're).

2. Look for homophones that spell check may not catch.

3. Read the paper backwards, one word at a time, to focus on individual words.

Capitalization

1. Ensure that the first word of every sentence is capitalized.

2. Check that proper nouns (names, places, specific titles) are correctly capitalized.

3. Verify correct capitalization of titles according to the chosen formatting style (e.g., MLA, APA).

Omissions

1. Check for missing words that affect the meaning of sentences.

2. Ensure that every sentence has a subject and a verb.

3. Read sentences aloud or have someone else read them to catch missing words.

Punctuation

1. Check for missing or incorrect punctuation, such as commas, periods, apostrophes, and quotation marks.

2. Ensure proper use of semicolons, colons, and dashes where needed.

3. Watch for comma splices and run-on sentences.

Ear (Listening for Clarity and Flow)

1. Read the paper aloud to hear how it flows and to identify awkward phrasing.

2. Ask a peer to read the paper aloud to get a different perspective on clarity and coherence.

3. Break up overly long sentences to improve readability and avoid confusion.

Final Checklist

After applying the SCOPE editing process, ask yourself the following questions:

- Does my paper effectively convey my argument?
- Is my writing clear, concise, and well-organized?
- Have I checked for grammar and citation errors?

By following SCOPE, you ensure that your writing is polished, professional, and ready for submission.

www.ingramcontent.com/pod-product-compliance
Lightning Source LLC
Chambersburg PA
CBHW072236290326
41934CB00008BB/1315